Philosophy
in the
Dungeon

The Magic of Sex & Spirit

Philosophy
in the
Dungeon
The Magic of Sex & Spirit

Jack Rinella

Foreword by Dossie Easton

Rinella Editorial Services

Published by
Rinella Editorial Services
4205 North Avers Avenue
Chicago, IL 60618 USA

www.RinellaEditorial.com

Book and Cover designs and Illustrations
by
Michael Tallgrass

Contact him at mtallgrass@aol.com

Library of Congress Control Number: 2006905166

ISBN 0-940267-10-1

Printed in the United States of America

To Liam and Quinn

That they may know what their

Grandfather believed

Table of Contents

Author's Note

Before you purchase or read this book there are a few things you ought to know:

This book is neither an introductory volume on being kinky nor a book about SM techniques, but let me quickly assure you that you can still enjoy this book if alternate sexual practices are new territory to you. If you are not an experienced Bondage/Discipline/Domination/Submission/Sadism/Masochism (BDSM) player, then I suggest that you avail yourself of one or two of the titles listed in the appendix under Suggested Reading, before you attempt to have kinky sex.

Philosophy In the Dungeon is filled with ideas that some people consider dangerous, some heretical, some Satanic, and some just downright foolish. With the exception of the dangerous part, I don't agree with any of those detractors.

As for what's dangerous, I can take no responsibility for your irresponsible behavior. I am not urging you to do anything that I've done. Additionally, no one should attempt any sexual practices without full knowledge of how to do them safely, sanely, and consensually. Some things that kinky folks do should only be done when they have gained the proper expertise.

Cultures that routinely practice "Magic" have developed rather sophisticated safeguards to protect themselves, those who practice it, and those upon whom it is practiced. This is not, then, a complete "How-to" nor a fully-referenced manual. It is the candid telling of my experiences and my beliefs, i.e., the Philosophy I learned in the dungeon. There are many who call themselves magicians -- and they quite well may be -- who would also have me tell you that practicing magic can be dangerous when done by the ignorant and that, like SM, you ought to learn from an expert before you attempt it. There are some, in fact, who will condemn this book for telling secrets that they think the average person shouldn't know.

My personal philosophy is that "All will be revealed" and that the "Truth will set you free." You will note as you read this book that I don't have much to hide. In any case I urge you to play safely and act responsibly.

As you read these pages you'll see symbols in the margin (as on the left) which mark "Key Ideas." I've marked them as such because they reflect the basics of what I believe. Together they add up to the paradigms I hold to be true.

That said, I trust you will enjoy this book.

Jack Rinella

Foreword

W hat you have just opened is an amazing book about spiritual consciousness, everyday metaphysics, faith -- and sex. Author Jack Rinella generously shares with us his path of revelation from his years as an aspiring priest to his coming out as a gay leatherman, still teaching spiritual practice, still seeking spiritual truth.

With utterly no apologies, Rinella takes on the difficult task of reuniting sex and spirituality, which have been so painfully severed over the last few hundred years of European cultural and religious history. He courageously refuses to compartmentalize or to shroud his lifestyle in the closet: after all, how could anyone write a book about the fundamental unity of everything in spirit and leave out sex?

In a society which pathologizes and even criminalizes explorers in the realms of sex and S/M, open discussions of our sexual experience are often considered somehow invalid and unsafe. But I know from experience that the real danger is that when we refuse to speak openly -- and proudly -- about our sex lives, we consign ourselves and our children to a jungle of unconscious reactivity, where men are taught to steal sex and women to hoard it, and sex is devalued as "worldly" and robbed of the spirit that should be the animating force in our intimate connections.

Jack, on the other hand, turns constantly to his many sexual journeys as the source of luminous truths, including his process of coming out into his own light as a gay man, and into his

S/M lifestyle. He states, brilliantly, that our "lifestyle is always an expression of salvation." He expands our understanding of faith as an omnipresent force in our everyday lives and simultaneously shows us how faith stretches far beyond our imaginations. He leads us into mystery as he states: "the truth I seek is broader than I will ever comprehend."

He encourages us to get disillusioned -- what good are illusions anyway? He shows us how to live and love rooted firmly in the present, and reminds us that every "voyage is greater than the destination". As he deconstructs the perils of orthodoxy, he encourages us to increase the flow of energy in our sex lives by recognizing that sex is neither a brainless nor a soulless activity, but a very sweet way of surrendering to spirit.

Ultimately, Jack Rinella charges us with a mission -- to live our lives authentically in unity with ourselves and our beliefs, and to let our entire lives, and especially our sex lives, be an expression of our spirit and a constantly renewing source of revelation. Thank you, Jack, you are an inspiration.

Dossie Easton
Licensed Marriage and Family Therapist
Co-author, with Janet Hardy, of:
> *The New Bottoming Book*
> *The New Topping Book*
> *The Ethical Slut*
> *When Someone You Love Is Kinky*
> *Radical Ecstasy: S/M Journeys to Transcendence*
And a proud and active sex radical since 1961.

Introduction

As I reflect on the content of this book, I can only marvel at the changes I have undergone in life. It was only 25 years ago, for instance, that I was baptized by immersion in the pond of a charismatic Jesus People commune. Then again, only four years earlier I had been a devout Roman Catholic college student studying for ordination as a priest. In the years since then I have found myself attending classes in Transcendental Meditation, researching phallic worship, seeking to learn how to do "sex magic," and actively writing and speaking nationally in the subculture of alternate sexuality, variously called the "lifestyle," "Leather," and "kink."

What has been consistent has been a search for meaning and the truth of what it means to be fully human, especially within the context of spirituality. This book, then, is an attempt to express what I have experienced and, through those experiences, learned. *Philosophy In the Dungeon* is my reflection on that quest and an attempt to arrive at a meaningful understanding of what it means to be human.

As a kinky and sexually active man who has lived a life filled with spiritual experience and religious study, I am all too aware of the tension between holiness, as defined by mainline contemporary religions, and sexual activity, especially of the radical and promiscuous type. Most religious leaders, after all, spend much more time condemning sexual activity than extolling its virtue and its sacredness. I also understand that for many the world of magic is thought to be either evil or foolish and that it

1

certainly has no place in one's bedroom.

For me, sexual bliss and religious ecstasy are one and the same experience. The body and its functions are as holy as the soul. Physical love and divine love are identical in nature. What is magical is simply what is. The tensions between flesh and spirit are man-created, not having any reality outside of a guilty and shame-ridden psyche.

I write then to resolve those tensions, attempting to find holiness in wholeness and worship in its fullness. The resolution of all tension is found in harmony, which is the very state to which I hope this book will lead.

About Me

When I wrote a short biography of myself in the fall of 1996 I realized that the one repeating focus in my life was my quest for spiritual understanding. Having had a large assortment of occupations, no one place where I had lived for very long, having been divorced, and having spent most of my life either underemployed or involved in some alternative lifestyle, one could look at me and see a person who was continually discontented. In fact, in 1965 the rector of Mater Christi Seminary, which I was attending at the time, asked me why I seemed so dissatisfied with life.

In the course of my 59 years of living, I have been Roman Catholic, Pentecostal, the pastor of a Congregational Church, and a New Age student and meditator. I have considered myself Jewish (for one night at least), a neo-Pagan, a Dionysian, a Gnostic, and a man who just didn't have a religious clue. In all of this there are strong indications of a great deal of searching and not a lot of finding. Yet this open-hearted experimentation is the strong evidence of a deep hunger, quest if you will, to know God and to understand life, thereby being able to live it deeply and fully.

What is added to this mix is my full participation in Gay (though I probably qualify as a bisexual), sadomasochistic, and dominant/submissive sexuality. For the many believers of a wide variety of traditional doctrines, a spiritual life and a sexually active one seem to be at loggerheads. In our culture, penance, fasting, hair shirts, and abstinence are thought to be more akin to holiness than are hedonism and sexual liberation. I, on the other hand, have experienced the deeply moving visitation of divinity in what some would call promiscuity and sexual depravity. The white light that appeared to me while attending Mass as an adolescent (circa 1958) and the white light I experienced in a sadomasochistic leather scene in 1985 were very much one and the same experience. (More on this later.)

On other hand, I cannot satisfactorily explain the nature and meaning of those lights. My vocabulary is too limited, my intelligence too small to grasp the width, depth, and height of the infinite, omnipotent, omnipresent, and all-knowing. Take those words as a warning. I'm no expert in divinity, in eternity, nor in much of anything. I am a fallible and culpable human.

I can only attempt to move one small step forward toward more light. This book is my invitation to you to see the sacredness of sex and its spiritual possibilities. It is my attempt to understand why and how sex is holy, beautiful and good-to-experience. Herein I will not show you **the way,** but I trust my experiences and insights might help you to "Know, love, and serve God in this world and to be happy with Him in the next" -- just as I was taught in first grade.

An Eclectic Approach

If I were still in grammar school, I'd be accused (OK, diagnosed) as having attention deficit disorder. Happily I graduated from eighth grade long before the social scientists took over the work of the nuns. The truth is that I prefer to work on several projects at a time and my attention on any one project wanes quickly. That being the case, I'm a natural candidate for being eclectic. You'll find herein all sorts of pieces from various disciplines. My approach to spirituality is a medley, a stew, a mosaic.

I believe that truth exists in many places and is best found through the use of many disciplines and methodologies. There is a way for each of us, but probably not one path for all of us. Our uniqueness, our individuality points each of us in a highly personalized direction. There are many roads and all of them lead to Rome, though not necessarily to Rome in Italy. All disciplines hold and reveal some truth, but none have all of it. For that reason the first four chapters may seem unrelated. The first chapters of this book consider the idea of time and paradigms, the body and the mind, historical theologies, and the body as an energetic entity. Then we'll pause to reflect on how these four topics affect my consideration of sex and spirit. Moving then from general reflection to a discourse on unity and then on human life, we will finally consider the possibility of a spiritual life practiced in a subculture of kink and sex, which leads naturally to the techniques of what many call magic.

So with a bit of this and bit of that I invite you to join me in a search for enlightenment. Let our paths merge for this part of the journey, knowing that each of us has the responsibility to listen not only to the other but especially to the small silent voice of one's own soul, which of course is the most important voice of all.

The Necessity of Wholeness

For whatever reason we only see darkly and do not see the whole. Yes we may know one side of the coin well; still the other is out of sight. We can grasp pieces but never the entirety, hence our understanding is always incomplete. Still there is the necessity to recognize that wholeness exists, even if the full knowledge of it presently evades us.

This notice, then, serves as a warning that this book is and will be incomplete. No surprise there. It also reminds us that we have to keep in mind that there is a wholeness to be sought. The trap is that we get caught in a perspective, in a limited mode of understanding, and thereby disregard other modes that have something to teach us as well. Our culture thrives on the expertise of specialists and does so for good reason. Yet there is the constant need to approach answers fully in a generalist's sort of way, meaning that we seek the full answer.

This is what is called an holistic approach. The word reminds us to seek wholeness and holiness; true holiness being none other than wholeness itself. Our search, then, is many-faceted: physical, emotional, intellectual, spiritual, communal, solitary, financial, legal, social, familial, interior, outward, etc. I write this to remind us that no one chapter, no one approach is going to satisfy the whole person – and in the end, satisfaction, complete satisfaction, being fully filled, is our goal. As you read, then, the following chapters, try to see each of them as part of a whole.

They are separated for good pedagogy and because we can communicate only in categories. It is by dividing the whole into parts that we can comprehend it. There is no other way for us to learn. In reality the parts are never separate. They only appear to be such. They are all connected, even when the connections are so fine that we miss them entirely.

How the Book Is Put Together

I tried to take a rather orderly approach to the topic of kinky sex, spirituality, and magic so the book begins with four topics that seem unrelated: paradigms, certain aspects of our physical nature, ancient cultures and their religions, and what we call the power exchange. Though we seldom think of these subjects as related, they are. Unfortunately we seldom consider them when we discuss or ponder what it is that we do in the dungeon.

The paradigms (i.e., the patterned ways we view the world) which we hold affect our thoughts, our feelings, and our negotiations about kinky sex. After all, as my Mom would say, "I didn't raise you that way." Indeed many of our paradigms tell us what the rest of the world wants us to think about BDSM: Don't do it. Effective and satisfactory BDSM then needs to develop its own supportive paradigms.

There are times, of course, when we do consider our bodies, especially when our seminars turn to physical safety. How often, though, do we think about our physical reactions to bondage, impact play, or any scene that leads to "subspace?" (A blissful, calm experience induced in many different ways.) Indeed, subspace is just as much a physical experience as any other type.

We fully admit that we kinky folk form a subculture. As such we also think of what we do as being alternative, if not counter-culture. Therefore considering ancient cultures that significantly differ from the predominant American culture in which we find ourselves is meant to be liberating, freeing us to more fully consider what it is we do, without the baggage of the primary culture (or at least with less of it), because we realize that other peoples in other times and places thought and behaved differently.

And lastly, a study of human life as an energy flow begins to explain what we do when we exchange power. The experience of energy is, after all, more than just a euphemism. In any case, as I unfold my Philosophy In the Dungeon, each of these topics will come together, leading to the chapter, "A Pause to Reflect."

From there we will explore unity, which is not only

the philosophical basis that makes this all "work" but also is the overwhelming experience found in any good BDSM scene. Whether we call it floating, bonding, or subspace, it is the strong feeling of oneness with the Universe and often the unstated goal of what it is that we do.

We then turn to "Life As Process" in order to develop a paradigm that allows for continued growth and development. The process paradigm gives meaning to being. Discovery of meaning is certainly a goal of Philosophy, even a kinky philosophy. If there is process then there are stages. Understanding this, we can better understand how our kink grows and changes as it affects us.

Fundamental to the development of Magic, the practitioner has to believe. Doing so, though, is not an easy task for many BDSM players as the paradigms of those of the predominant faiths often condemn, ostracize, and negate our lifestyle. The "According To Your Faith" chapter, then, is meant to give us a new view of faith, one that is supportive of kink and the unique expression of faith that we practice.

But faith can lead to dogmatism, self-righteousness, and intolerance, all of which will eventually destroy our practice of BDSM. Before we proceed, therefore, it is wise to develop a spirituality that is true and from there to manifest it practically. Having done these things the stage is set for a fuller understanding of the way we create, which leads to Magic, a more intense form of creating.

Read on, then, kinky folks, and discover as best you can the deep truths of what it is that we do. Remember, though, that I am a fellow traveler and that no book can contain the Universe we discover in the dungeon. With that important caveat let us begin.

Chapter 1

In the Beginning

Both the Book of Genesis and the Gospel According to John start with the words "In the beginning." Those words come naturally as an appropriate way to start either the narrative of the creation of the world or the pre-eminence of Christ. Unfortunately, "In the beginning" in itself expresses a paradigm, in this case a particular way of looking at the world. The phrase assumes that there was a beginning to the universe, as if at one point in time there was no world and then at some mysterious moment, in some inexplicable way, the world sprang into existence. The unspoken assumption is that creation had a beginning.

More importantly, the phrase implies a linear approach to creation. If there was a beginning, then there is a middle, and will be an end. The New Testament seems to explicitly posit in several different places, and especially in a literal reading of The Book of the Apocalypse also attributed to John, that the world will come to an end. A linear view of history is one of the hallmarks of Western (European) thinking. We see history as a progressive unfolding, a constant improvement, leading to some future state of completion.

Eastern cultures have a different world view, seeing creation as cyclical, as exemplified in the spinning prayer wheels of Tibetan monks. In that view, the world revolves through stages of creation, existence, transformation, and re-creation, much more akin to the cycles of the seasons, ever repetitive, and ever-renewing.

"In the beginning" may not be the only or best translation; it might not be anything more than an obvious way

9

to start a story. In Robert Alter's translation of the first five books of the Old Testament, he renders the same phrase as "When God began,"[1] thus emphasizing the eternal nature of God, though still alluding to the linear nature of Hebraic history.

In spite of this point, I have no quarrel with the idea of "beginning." Instead, I want to point out what seems to be the best starting point for any consideration of spirit: we need to understand that each of us, myself included, perceives, interprets, and acts according to the paradigms that influence our ability to perceive, interpret, and act.

Paradigm means "example, pattern," and so refers to the patterns that we observe and use as the basis for our comprehension of reality. In this case, Westerners see the pattern of positive change throughout the millennia and conclude that existence is linear, while Easterners see the repetitive nature of life and conclude that there is a cyclical pattern intrinsic to it. In each case the conclusion then leads to fundamental and essentially different ways of thinking.

Paradigms greatly affect our perspective, as they form the basis of our ability to understand and communicate. If we believe that the history of the world is linear, we automatically interpret world events in that light. It is as if each of us wears rose-colored glasses and therefore all that we see has a rose tint to it. The glasses are so fundamental to our perception that we don't even know we are wearing them. One could make the case that there is no way to remove the tint, that our perceptions are fundamentally and inescapably colored by our experiences, our basic thought processes, and even the limitations of the languages we speak.

Culture, "The totality of socially transmitted behavior patterns, arts, beliefs, institutions, and all other products of human work and thought,"[2] transmits its paradigms to its members as it

socializes them into itself, a process that begins at birth. Each of us, then, is indelibly formed by the culture in which we are born and the subcultures in which we live, even if that formation leads to a later rejection of that culture and the creation of an alternative one.

In the same way that culture influences our perceptions it influences "all other products of human work and thought" including any understanding we have of the concepts of spirit, the divine, and human existence. Religion, law, our perception of physical reality, prejudice, and even ignorance are all products of one's culture. There is no escaping its effects. We can only attempt to somehow include a consideration of them in our reasoning processes, which are themselves naturally influenced by culture.

Even as I write this book, which many will find espouses beliefs that are contradictory to the Italian-American, Roman Catholic culture of my youth, I am influenced by one of the earliest dogmas I was taught: "Q. Why did God make you? A. God made me to know Him, to love Him, and to serve Him in this world, and to be happy with Him forever in heaven."[3] I cannot escape that which has made me who I am. The best I can hope for is to understand all that makes me who I am and to deal with those influences appropriately.

In the same way, when I write "There is no escaping its effects," I am reflecting a paradigm, in this case one that could be called agnostic, that is the belief that says that I cannot know. Paradoxically as you read further you will find that I espouse the opposite paradigm as well, as I am very much gnostic, that is, I believe that we can know.

Paradigms and BDSM

As I noted in the Introduction, I wasn't raised to be kinky. Chances are you weren't, either. So we come to "the scene" with beliefs that we will, in fact, have to change if we are to become fully developed and well-balanced players. Think for a moment of the paradigms you once held (and may still) that warn you to stay away from people like us and to never do what it is that we do.

I have a vivid recollection of the night I had to fully face one of those paradigms. I was topping an experienced masochist in my small basement dungeon in Ft. Wayne. We had met a month or so before and his ability to take pain attracted me. I had come to learn that for reasons that still escape me, sadistic activity is a strong turn-on for me. Not only does being sadistic stiffen my prick, I find great pleasure in inflicting pain on a willing partner.

I had him tied spread eagle and face down on a mattress on the floor, while I knelt in front of him, his head between my knees. I warmed his back and butt with the strokes of several different floggers and eventually proceeded to use a rather severe buggy whip, raising bright red streaks on his body.

At some point, while I was enjoying the scene immensely, I remembered the nuns' teaching me not to hit another person. As the whip struck him, I was blatantly struck by the paradigm of "Thou shalt not kill," and all the moral implications of what I was doing. Then and there, as the whip landed on my partner I had to choose between the paradigm from grade school or a new one. In short order I realized that what I was doing had nothing in common with the nuns' proscriptions. My activity was both consensual and non-aggressive.

I continued the beating, knowing that my partner was enduring a rite of passage into a deep and blissful subspace, even as I was experiencing the passage into the deeper understanding of Leather sex and a more BDSM-friendly paradigm.

As the pain I inflicted wrought its magic, he became silent, surrendering to each stroke. In due time I knew that we had created an experience of great depth and feeling. Only later did I learn that he had left his body on the mattress and in his mind's eye risen to the rafters of the dungeon to watch what was transpiring. For him it was an ecstatic experiencing. For me it was the beginning of a way of understanding that would change many paradigms and then my life.

The Many Ways of Knowing

As in the different historical perspectives mentioned above there are many other ways that one develops an understanding of spirit: agnostic or gnostic; Apollonian or Dionysian; hedonistic or puritanical; spiritualistic or materialistic. Each perspective represents a paradigm that likewise tints our views. We may think that we arrive at one or another of these views as a consequence of reason or experience but nevertheless all conclusions are first based on some kind of assumption, which is another way of stating that we are wearing rose-colored glasses.

These "glasses" serve as a metaphor for our native inability to fully comprehend divinity and the realm of spirit. Our intellectual capabilities, as of yet, are still under-developed. We, the finite, cannot understand the breadth and height of the infinite; we, the temporal, have no way to comprehend the eternal; in our physical and mortal flesh we cannot truly know the everlasting and ever-living.

Yes, faith is a way of knowing each of these aspects of other-than-us, but it is faith, not reasoned or experiential knowledge. This is not to demean faith, as it is a necessary and ever-present fact of human existence. It is only to recall that faith is its own kind of surety, neither experiential nor scientific, and that we use faith to prove faith. Still within us is the desire to know and to be known, to embrace the divine and to dwell within its safe embrace, even if the task is daunting and overwhelming.

The glass of water can know, in some way, the water which it holds, yet it can never hold and therefore know the ocean. Such is our fate. Let us try then to know that which we can, and trust that in some way, on some day, all will be revealed.

13

Reflecting on Philosophy In the Dungeon

The French call an orgasm "Le petit mort," the little death. If your experience of orgasm is anything like mine then you understand why that name is used. In the most intense moments of sexual activity, there is a suspension of the sense of time. We lose all counting of the seconds, and our concentration upon everything and anything disappears. Here then is the first event wherein we glimpse our participation in the eternal, the timeless, the ever-present now.

In the afterglow of the orgasm itself there is a less intense form of this experience of eternity, if we but let ourselves bask in the moment. Too often, of course, we don't. Instead we move to grab a towel, pleasure our partner, smoke a cigarette, or just plain fall asleep. If, instead, we and our partners were to allow ourselves to be more mindful, this glimpse into eternity could be prolonged at least long enough to teach us that time as we know it in the mundane world may not be as solid and demanding as we think.

1 Alter, Robert, *The Five Books of Moses*, W. W. Norton & Company, New York, 2004, page 17.

2 All definitions are taken from *Webster's Seventh New Collegiate Dictionary*, G&C Merriam Company, Springfield, MA, 1963.

3 *Baltimore Catechism No. 1*, found at http://www.catholic.net/rcc/Catechism/download/baltimore1.doc on September 24, 2005.

It's All in Your --- **2**

The first way that we'll look at sex and spirit is in the physical aspects of the brain, an approach that probably isn't taken very often by theologians, but one which is necessary if our discussion is going to be truly holistic.

I was going to start this chapter with the title "It's All in Your Brain," but as I began writing I realized that it's not all in our brains. Rather all of it, whatever "it" might be, may well be found throughout our bodies, the spaces we inhabit, in our histories, our cultures, indeed, throughout the universe. I'll let you decide where it *all* resides. Still, I begin by considering the brain because that is where it appears that perception is perceived, though other cultures might posit that it is not in the brain but in the heart. In our Western view what we sense by sight, touch, or any of the other senses is realized in our brains -- or to state it more correctly -- in our minds.

True spirituality needs to be holistic and therefore is a spirituality of the body as well as of the soul, a spirituality as applicable to earth as to heaven, to life as to the afterlife. In fact biological processes are as much a part of the discovery of the divine as are psychology, theology, philosophy, or extrasensory perception. There is as much to be learned about God in the bushes that grow and flower as there is in the burning bush from which the voice of God spoke to Moses.

If we are to believe the story in Isaiah where God spoke not in the clap of thunder or the roar of the wind but in the soft voice of the quiet breeze, then we can also accept the fact that when our brains are quieted from the chatter of everyday and mundane living, then we can best hear the quiet voice of the divine. Indeed meditation, relaxation, and the "spaces" of a BDSM scene all share the phenomenon of a decrease in brain wave activity. This then points to one way of understanding spiritual experiences and the practice of a spiritual life.

Please note that I said "one," not "only." We all live as a manifestation of many states of being, those many states comprising the unity, the single being that each of us calls "self." Even naming a "self" belies the fact that there is much to each of us that is hidden, subconscious, so that we don't fully know the "self" that each of us actually is.

That noted, the best way to approach living, to discuss that "self," is holistically. The fact that I am writing about a particular aspect of living is not meant to imply that it is the only or even the most important one.

The Mind's Place in All This

Much about effective BDSM occurs (as does everything else) as a result of good mind work, of proper attitude if you like, by the players. For the top that means that he or she guides the scene with good planning, good observation and correct technique, being especially aware of the bottom's head space while consciously encouraging the bottom to use his or her mind to control or not control the scene.

For the bottom it's necessary to use the mind to listen to one's inner self and then direct it and the other aspects of one's being in a manner that reflects one's goals, aspirations, and desires for the scene, even if the only goal is to have fun. That last sentence is filled with a great deal that needs explaining.

16

For starters, the bit about listening to one's inner self means that any activity ought to be consistent with what one knows to be one's authentic self. There's nothing that ruins a scene faster than pretense. For better or for worse, if one can't fully embrace an activity, then one is asking for a less-than-desirable encounter when one allows that activity.

Now there are times, of course, when half a loaf is better than none. There are scenes in which we willingly participate which may not be exactly what we want. There have been things I have done, for instance, which were meant to satisfy my partner but really didn't turn me on. In other cases, such as when I underwent a scene with sounds[1] inserted into my urethra, I only did so for the experience, certainly not for the pleasure. On the other hand it is just simple fact that there are times when the phrase "No thank you," is the best of all safe words.

Going forward then, we need to know what is meant by the word "mind," which for our purposes is best defined as "The totality of conscious and unconscious processes of the brain and central nervous system that directs the mental and physical behavior of a sentient organism." The mind, then, controls, (or ought to) the behavior, i.e., actions, reactions, emotions, movements, speech, feelings, etc. of mind's owner.

In a consensual BDSM encounter, there is no "mind control" by others in a Svengali or Manchurian Candidate sense.

But there certainly is a place, in fact an important one, for tops to aid their bottoms by encouragement, instruction, motivation, distraction, and reinforcement. These activities do not so much control the mind of the other as they support the other's control of his or her own mind. So, for instance, I may remind the cocksucker who is gagging on my dick to breathe or I may tell my flogged bottom that they are doing a good job and ought to easily take another ten on their red and sore back. The place of the mind in this is to direct the rest of one's being into a space which facilitates the desired result.

17

Lest the word "space" not be understood, let me suggest that in this case it means the mental process which leads to behavior. Even if that behavior is simply one manifested by a good attitude, all behavior is eventually demonstrated by appropriate action. The mind, therefore, may tell the body to relax as that paddle hits the ass cheek for the 237th time, having raised a nice red blister which is about to burst or as that tit clamp bites harder than one likes for the moment. It is the mind that directs one's being to surrender, to receive without complaint, to act in a specific way rather than react in what might be a more expected way.

We naturally expect that our reactions will be reflexive and spontaneous, even though the modus operandi of BDSM is for the mind to overcome "natural" reactions, such as pulling away or resisting, and instead act in ways to enhance the activity. It is the mind that tells the rest of one's being to relax, breathe, loosen up, accept, surrender, trust, and even to deny thoughts and actions that would negate the BDSM activity. This often means that the bottom has to use his or her mind to counteract the effect of fear, overcoming it so as to more fully participate in the event. This is where mind is best suited to foster a good scene.

It also means that our mind needs to be "at work" at times other than in the scene. Mind is needed during negotiations. It takes mind to analyze one's fears in order to understand and control them, something that may best be done well before the scene, or after it in preparation for the next one. Fears are a big factor in failed scenes, as is a lack of full agreement on what the scene is meant to achieve. Only by approaching both fears and negotiations with a fully engaged mind are we able to best enjoy the experience of what it is that we do.

It is therefore imperative that the mind be engaged even at times when there is no scene. This is the value of reflection, of discussion with others after the scene in some kind of review and analysis, and of understanding oneself, one's motivations, and one's expectations. It is especially important that fears be understood and seen as good and necessary, or as detracting and irrelevant. Being inhibited by unrealistic fears, for instance, is not helpful; being protected by fully rational ones is.

This understanding implies that we know ourselves and what we want, two other aspects that involve our mind. Therein lies an interesting contradiction. In the best of scenes we use our mind to enter what appears to be a mindless state of ecstasy, one where we drift into a delightful place devoid of consideration of body, soul, emotion, or mind. This is a place of such unity that intellectual compartmentalization becomes meaningless; we use the mind to lose, for the moment, all thought of mind, entering fully into the experience of one's true unity of self with the universe. There is more to this process than simply the physical activity of the fetish itself.

Entering either subspace or topspace is an important part of what we want to accomplish. Ought we not, then, to know what it is, how it works, and the ways that the process itself can be enhanced? I'd also like to note that topspace, a subject much less discussed, is probably the same phenomenon, though the physical aspects of its attainment are probably less known and even less understood.

It is in the sub- and topspace experience that we find the most obvious and direct connection between the physical and the mental, the body and the spirit, the sexual and the spiritual. The space that one experiences in the best of BDSM activity is very much like the sublime peace of the holiest raptures of religious experience.

Our Bodies & BDSM

This connection, this similarity, is exactly why I begin this book with an exploration of bodily functions such as brain waves and endorphins. There is no denying that the similarity of "religious" ecstasy and sexual orgasm is obvious. (St. Theresa comes to mind here.) In fact only the most anti-religious or anti-sexual minds would insist on there being a fundamental difference between them. Understanding the physical aspects of ecstasy is the first step in understanding the emotional, spiritual, and theological aspects of the same (even if differently-labeled) experience.

In any case, knowing what physically happens in the brain during a scene is a part of understanding the process in all its dimensions. Remember, please, that the value I place on understanding is not simply that we understand, but rather that increased understanding enhances the experience itself. My opinion is that if we know what's going on we can then encourage the process with appropriate responses.

Brain Waves

Let me begin with an elementary presentation on brain waves. Electroencephalograph machines are used by biologists and physicians to study and measure brain wave activity. The waves themselves are measured in terms of hertz (cycles per second. A hertz equals one cycle per second.), and are named as beta (14-30 hertz), alpha (9-13 hertz), theta (4-8 hertz), and delta (1-3 hertz).[2] (See illustration number one).

Beta waves indicate normal brain wave activity as in thinking, writing, or working. The higher the number of cycles per second, the more active the brain. Frenzied activity would be in the upper 20 hertz range.

As we relax, our brain waves slow down into the alpha range, such as when we are watching television or listening to relaxing music. Increased relaxation decreases brain wave activity into the theta range, which is often a state of reverie, where we find ourselves more creative. It is a day-dreaming state where thoughts flow easily and comfortably, as if we are dreaming. Passing through theta brings us to delta -- sleep.

We can describe a BDSM scene in terms of brain wave

activity. In fact I would love to have a neurologist record brain wave activity during a scene to confirm my suspicions. Alas, few scientists venture into our dungeons with their research equipment!

Obviously we are in beta when we negotiate and then begin a scene. The warming up at the beginning of a scene is meant to move the participants from beta to alpha. Most players, then, spend their time in an alpha state, except when one or both

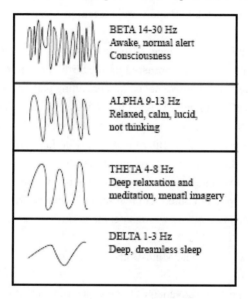

	BETA 14-30 Hz Awake, normal alert Consciousness
	ALPHA 9-13 Hz Relaxed, calm, lucid, not thinking
	THETA 4-8 Hz Deep relaxation and meditation, menatl imagery
	DELTA 1-3 Hz Deep, dreamless sleep

Illustration Number One.[3]

is able to move into what is sometimes called "theta reverie." This seems to be easier for bottoms than for tops, since tops generally have to maintain a level of awareness in order to do what they are doing. Expert tops, of course, can and do enter theta if their technique is such that it is as natural to them as driving a car five miles down a familiar freeway.

What is important here is to see the connections between what we do in the dungeon and what we do everywhere else, therefore being able to use non-BDSM techniques to enhance our kinky experiences. It is my experience that bondage, flogging, whipping, fisting, fucking, needle play, and the like all have the potential of altering our brain wave patterns.

There are, too, other processes that do the same thing. Immersion in any activity, especially an artistic one, will have a similar effect. Meditating, listening to music, and certain breathing exercises are other processes that have a similar effect. Might we not, then, use both kinky and vanilla techniques to double our pleasure?

I think, for instance, of the lessons I learned at Lamaze classes as my wife and I prepared for the birth of our first child. It was there that I learned that certain breathing patterns would reduce the effect of pain. Later at the New Age center where I learned to meditate, I was taught that muscle relaxation and/or visualization would do similar things to my brain's activity.

In the dungeon, in my quiet times, when writing, similar processes are occurring. Lessons learned in one venue can and should be applied in others. A great scene is what we're seeking, isn't it? Let's find all the ways to get there.

The Mind-Body Connection

One of the advantages to being a writer is that I get plenty of time to think philosophically about what it is that we do. I strongly suggest that this kind of rumination is not appropriate during a scene, as cerebral commentary about what is happening is not very conducive to sex. While care and thought should always go into what we are doing, and tops in particular must be thinking about technique and safety, in sexual scenes we desire blissful abandon, not critical analysis.

In my quest to become fully human, I have done a lot of thinking about Metaphysics, which was actually a course I took as a Philosophy major in college. For me, the question has usually boiled down to "How does the world work?" The optimistic assumption I am making is that if I knew in which order I should be pushing the universe's buttons, I could solve all of my problems, becoming handsome, wealthy, healthy, and a fully happy genius just by pushing those buttons.

Is it no wonder that I consider myself a dreamer of substantial proportions? Yet the years have shown me a small part of the wisdom of the ages, even if that gives me only enough knowledge to be dangerous. My mom might even say "Too smart for your own good." Nevertheless there is some satisfaction in having some of the loaf rather than none. That written, I will also remind you that my tentative conclusions are highly eclectic and very personal. They work for me and I think that is a good start. It is your responsibility to see if my conclusions will work for you.

I see a tremendous value in our understanding the connections between our minds and our bodies. In other words, what we think and feel has a significant impact on how we act and how our physical bodies respond. Likewise the converse is true. Our physical bodies and the messages they send to our brains greatly impact how we think and what we do. Understanding the connections between mind and body allows us to use them to our benefit.

An important assumption in all of this is that we have the ability to control ourselves. Too often we fail to acknowledge that we are responsible for how we think and how we feel. That's not to say that fleeting thoughts and immediate emotional reactions spring from our wills, but rather that we have the power to decide when and how we will respond to them. For instance, an event may anger me. I then have the opportunity to choose to become violent or to redirect that anger into a more constructive reaction.

One of the things we do when we have a scene is to take advantage of our mind-body feedback loop. As we begin, our mind assents to certain things, such as being bound in rope

23

or having a spanking to warm us up. Our body, not detecting anything physically wrong, reacts only mildly to the sensations. Yes, it communicates to our mind that "There is a piece of rope on our wrist" or "Something is hitting our ass," but it does so without a major sense of distress. In any case, the mind sends back the message that "All is well; this is a consensual event."

Note a difficulty in this prose. Stating it as I have, it sounds as if the mind and the body are two entities, sharing a proximate space but somehow separate. Such is certainly not the case, but their communication is hard to explain without this. In any case remember that we are unified beings.

In due time our physical selves will begin to feel that our mental selves have gone mental. "Wait a minute," the body will say, "that hurt." The mind, of course, will continue to try its best to calm the body. It will tell itself to relax, to breathe, not to worry. Additionally it will refuse to send messages to the mouth to yell "Stop. This hurts. I've changed my mind." In that way, then, the mind controls the body. To what end? It wants the body to cooperate with its desire to enter an altered state, either subspace or topspace.

In an effort to overcome the stress the mind is allowing to be placed on the body, our body will then react to the pain by releasing chemicals into the bloodstream, specifically endorphins, that will mitigate, block, and mask the pain. "Ah," thinks the mind, "the body is doing its job," since the endorphins have the added effect of giving the brain the good feelings it wanted when it allowed its body to be part of the scene. In actual practice, of course, the body is naturally conditioned to release these endorphins. The mental, physical, emotional, spiritual, chemical, and energetic aspects of what I just described are much more complex than I've stated but I hope they make my point.

We often simplify the discussion by referring to what is happening as a power exchange. (More on this later.) More specifically, in a scene we exchange power to move one another into different states of perceiving and feeling. Among other things, it changes the amplitude and frequency of our brain waves.

Focusing on brain wave activity is not meant to imply that a scene is merely about changing our brain waves. I don't think that beginning a negotiation by saying "Let's alter our brain wave patterns" is a very good place to start, though you may want to try it if your current approach isn't working.

Negotiation is the act of mutually deciding the hoped-for outcome of a scene or relationship. When it's successful, what ensues is the use of our minds and bodies to attain those goals. Most of the time, what we want to accomplish is simply to have a good time. We are all about fun, really. Still, over the course of time, there are lessons to be learned about ourselves and the universe while we are having fun.

The trick here, then, is to take the lessons learned on the cross, the bondage table, the bed, or in the dungeon to improve one's life in general. To that end, I've come to the conclusion that living the "lifestyle" really means that one has managed to take those lessons, that fundamental understanding learned through BDSM, and apply them to the rest of one's life. Living is, after all, a constant energy exchange.

Endorphins

Although I got a decent grade in high school biology, I haven't seriously studied the subject since then. In any case there was no discussion on endorphins in class. As a matter of fact it wasn't until I read Geoff Mains' remarkable book, *Urban Aboriginals*,[4] in the mid 80's that I learned of endorphins.[5] Today we kinky folk use the term rather frequently in our attempt to describe what happens when we do what it is that we do.

Just as we could, with proper equipment, measure brain waves, so can we measure the level of various chemicals in the bloodstream. As brain waves affect our attitude, endorphins

-- chemicals produced in the brain -- do the same. Endorphins are in the opiate class of hormones and are naturally-produced pain blockers.

By blocking pain endorphins create a sense of euphoria in the body. Depending upon the extent of pain, whether through trauma, injury, physical exertion, or a good sadomasochistic encounter, the rising endorphin levels give rise to a sense of peace and wellness, again not unlike that of the reverie of spiritual experience. So to the idea that brain waves affect how we feel, we can add that endorphins have an effect, one not unrelated to brain waves as noted above.

It is no coincidence that meditation such as practiced by Zen masters and Buddhist monks alters both brain wave activity and endorphin levels in the same way as noted previously. Can the connection between body and spirit be more obvious? Likewise sexual activity alters these phenomena, leading us again to the conclusion that there are myriad connections, a complete interrelatedness, in all aspects of what it means to be truly human.

Reflecting on Philosophy In the Dungeon

Although much has been written on the physical aspects of sex, we seldom discuss the physical aspects of spirituality. Permeated as our thinking is with the duality that mankind is composed of body and soul, perhaps it is necessary to appropriate other models, since the word "and" seems to separate rather than join. Let us rather reflect on the physicality of spirituality, that our physical and spiritual natures are intrinsically joined, inseparable for a long as we are living.

Let us consider man as matter, as spirit, as soul, as emotive entity and passion, as ego, as instinct and desire, as intelligent being. Brain waves and endorphins are only two aspects of our physical existence. We could consider ourselves dynamically (How do our muscles move our fingers?), as mass (How does gravity affect us?), as digestive process (How does food become bone, tissue, and hormone? What part of my next meal will become egg or sperm?), and so forth.

What, too, is the spirit of man? If it is some form of energy, how does it differ from light or heat? If it is some form of God, what does that mean? How, then, are the body and the soul connected through spirit? How is, if it is, spirit different from soul? Lastly, how does sex intersect with matter and spirit? Why and how is sex sacred and what does that mean?

1　　　Medical rods inserted into the urethra to clear or stretch it. An elongated instrument for surgically exploring body cavities.

2　　　For a fuller explanation see Appendix A.

3　　　Adapted from "http:// www.forum.hr/ showthread.php?t=130795"

4　　　Mains, Geoff, *Urban Aboriginals*, Daedalus Publishing, Los Angeles, 2004.

5　　　For a fuller explanation see Appendix B.

Chapter 3

Spirit As the Ancients Knew It

$\mathbf{H}$aving looked at our topic from a physical viewpoint, let us move on to explore an historical perspective. In doing so let me note that my extensive use of quotations in this chapter is simply a reflection that historians' knowledge forms an invaluable insight into spiritualities and sexualities that significantly differ from our own. Their collective perspective is richer than I can give alone.

Living as we do in a culture thoroughly immersed in a Judeo-Christian world-view, there is the refreshing possibility that by looking outside that paradigm, to one not yet affected by the Tribes of Judah or the teachings of Christ, we can gain a different perspective, new insights, and a hint of what it looks like outside of our own rose-tinted world. That's not to dismiss the importance of the teachings of the Jews or of the Christians but rather to see if we can learn more by looking at our subject from the eyes of different cultures, millennia, or places.

The difficulty of the translation from foreign and ancient languages weighs heavily on this approach, compounded by the genocide by Christians of "non-believers," the book-burnings and witch-hunts, the forced mass conversions, and the simple ravages of time.

The history I was taught, of course, was primarily the names and dates of those who were heroes to the culture in which I was raised. Steeped as I was in Roman Catholicism, my teachers labeled even commonly recognized Protestant faiths as heretical; all others were pagan, primitive, or downright Satanic. My fellow students and I were well-educated in the "One, holy, catholic, and apostolic" way, as if the God who created myriad varieties when it came to stars, flowers, and phenomena could only conceive one son, one way, and one truth.

This history reflects a paradigm which I believe needs to be challenged. By looking at other cultures we can gain insight into other perspectives and other world-views.

As I hope I've made clear, my path has become eclectic, multi-dimensional; the truth I seek is wider, broader, and deeper than I will ever be able to comprehend. Of course, this chapter, indeed this book, can be only a pale glimmer of Reality. "For our knowledge," as St. Paul wrote,

> is imperfect; but when the perfect comes, the imperfect will pass away. When I was a child, I spoke like a child, I thought like a child, I reasoned like a child; when I became a man, I gave up childish ways. For now we see in a mirror dimly, but then face to face. Now I know in part; then I shall understand fully, even as I have been fully understood. So faith, hope, love abide, these three; but the greatest of these is love."[1]

I've chosen a number of non-Christian religions, primarily from pre-Christian centuries, together with various works of literature that shed some light on them, as a starting point for a simple, but I hope effective, investigation of the intersection of spirit and sexuality. They are the Sumerians and the text of Gilgamesh, the Hindus of India and the Bhagavad Gita, the ancient Chinese with both the Way of Zen and the Tao (though I admit to using more contemporary commentaries here), the Ancient Greeks and the myth and cult of Dionysos, the monotheism of ancient Israel, and lastly Rome and its Mystery Schools.

It is painfully obvious from reading that list that other cultures, histories, and perspectives are left out. The teachings of

Northern Europeans, such as the Norse and Celtic traditions, of
Native Americans, and of both African and Aboriginal cultures can
also add greatly to this study and I encourage you to explore those
paths as well. I can only ask the forbearance and understanding of
those cultures not mentioned, and they are many.

Sumer

The Sumerian epic of Gilgamesh is one of the oldest
heroic epics known. The historical Gilgamesh was apparently a
Sumerian king of the Early Dynastic period, ruling circa 2700
B.C.E.[2] The text telling of his deeds was written in the first
millennium B.C.E., and consists of twelve tablets, the last of
which gives an alternate version of the death of Enkidu. It, in turn,
was based on an earlier epic written in the Old Babylonian period
(1800-1600 B.C.E.). In addition to the epic, there are several
Sumerian poems about incidents in Gilgamesh's career, produced
during the reign of Shulgi, around 2000 B.C.E.[3]

Located in the fertile crescent, between the Tiger and
Euphrates Rivers in what is now known as Iraq, the civilization
of Sumer, a group of loosely associated cities, is my starting point
because the epic of Gilgamesh is one of the few original myths of
ancient societies that has survived through the ages to come down
to us.

The epic itself, which I can hardly narrate justly in a
paragraph or two, concerns the priest-king Gilgamesh ("I am Ensi
of Erech, son of Lugalbanda and Rimsat-Ninsun, two-thirds god
and one-third man.") and his wife-priestess-goddess Shamhatu.
Early in the story the youthful Gilgamesh is shown as proud and
independent, refusing to do his priestly duty by marrying Shamatu.
Word comes to them of a wild man in the countryside who lives
with lions. In response to prophecy, Shamatu ventures to meet and
tame him, bringing him, Enkidu, back to their city. Gilgamesh
and Enkidu form a deep and homosexual friendship. For his part

Enkidu tempers Gilgamesh's legalism with a native sense of justice.

Together they reign and have several successful adventures, proving their might until Enkidu dies. In grief Gilgamesh attempts the most serious of all adventures, daring to travel to the underworld in search of his lost love. Failing to regain Enkidu, he returns to Erech, where he finally takes Shamatu as his wife and the city prospers.

The Sumerians worshipped a multitude of what we would now call fertility gods. Their temples housed sacred prostitutes (as we call them). In cities where the local deity was male, the prostitutes would have been male. Cities that worshipped goddesses favored female ones. The worshippers would pay them for their sexual service, which was seen as prayer and worship to the resident god(dess).

Sumerians thought that their deities enjoyed receiving such devotional activity. Indeed they were believed to have participated in the sexual act by inhabiting the body of the priest(ess). The myths of such peoples were full of sexual expression. Rain was thought to spring from the loins of the gods and to fertilize the land. The gods and goddesses were renowned for their sexual activity. Fertility was of the utmost importance to these people: of the land lest famine devastate them, of their flocks, and of themselves as children were needed for labor and for care of their parents in the parents' later years, and as many children were needed since so many died in their youth.

Today we would be horrified by the idea of having intercourse in church but that is exactly what these ancient societies practiced. This is how Stephan Grundy depicted it in his novelized version of Gilgamesh:

> But tonight is the night of the full moon;
> and, as darkness quickly falls and the moon rises
> in the heavens, we hear the sounds of hundreds of

priestesses, chanting dully and playing primitive pipes and drums. Dressed in elaborate ceremonial garb, they gather solemnly around the terrace on which the temple is built, looking upward to the stepped pyramid beyond the temple, which rises almost in defiance of geometry, almost (it seems) to the sky itself. At the highest platform of this ziggurat (for so the stepped pyramid is called) is a small but glowing altar of lapis lazuli, carved fantastically with snakes and giant spiders, to which an adolescent boy has been bound on his back. He is naked, though his flesh has been decorated in patterns of lozenges and zigzags to resemble the cobra. Priestesses of the highest order, also naked except for their extraordinary rings and spiral bracelets, are massaging the boy with gentle foreplay. As the moonlight illuminates his swelling member, the high priestess appears, as if from nowhere, dressed in a silver garment, which she sheds. Now naked, except for the myriad pearls that decorate her body and the painted spirals that adorn her breasts, she mounts the boy with the assistance of her sisters, who shriek their encouragement in a frenzy that only grows higher as the high priestess rides the boy, at first with rhythmic dignity, then with increasing agitation till her pearls tremble in the moonlight like so many minuscule planets, and the lozenges and spirals glisten, and both bodies, writhing in sweat, appear to be not so much earthly bodies as inhuman forces of the cosmos. All the priestesses, the lowest orders still on the terrace at the ziggurat's base, the higher orders arranged in ascending importance on the lofty steps of the ziggurat itself, are growing wild and ecstatic. Ripping open their robes and pawing themselves, they bay upward to the event on the ziggurat's height and to the moon itself.[4]

We don't really know what such sexual worship was like, though the above narrative could well be more accurate than we think. Throughout the ancient world we find hundreds of references to such sexual acts as being acts of the religious. Indeed they were very much prevalent before the spread of Christianity and its establishment as the state religion throughout the Roman Empire. It was hardly akin to prostitution as we know it. It was rather the meeting of man or woman with god.

As we can read in Grundy's version of *Gilgamesh*:

> Taking a long pull from the beer, the aromatic sweetness of malt mingled with dates sliding smoothly down his throat, Akalla began to tell his wife the tale of what he had seen as they ate. For once, Innashagga sat silent, her charcoal-rimmed eyes widening; she gasped as he spoke of the lions milling around the wild man without harming him, but said nothing more until he finished by telling her of his father's advice and what he meant to do.

> "It is good advice, surely," Innashagga mused. "But to ask for the temple's Shamhatu, in whose lap men seek the blessings of the goddess -- should I let my husband go alone among such priestesses? Will he come back to a simple girl from the country, when he has once tasted the offerings of the temple-women? Or will he, too, forsake the wilderness and his animals, and turn his face toward the town, his back to the smell of sheep and goats?"

> Akalla reached over the jug to stroke her soft black hair. "The priestesses of Inanna are not for me: they are women for kings and noblemen."

> "Not always so," Akalla's father interrupted. "But Innashagga, you need have no fear. They serve when there is great need, and when the price can be paid for calling the goddess; and that, I remember, comes dearly. In my twenty years in the temple of Inanna, I lay with a priestess only thrice, and that because the temple sheep were sickening and her blessing was needed there. Nor do they ensnare men with their charms: it is the goddess, not the woman, who comes to her lovers, for the priestess' hope of

34

love and wedding of her own is her offering to Inanna.
You need have no fear."

"Then go, with my full blessing, my
husband," Innashagga said. Even in the dim light,
Akalla could see the tears welling in her dark eyes. He
did not know what to say, but he took her soft plump
hand and held it against his breast so she could feel
the beating of his heart.[5]

It is this understanding of the essential integrity of sexual
experience and a spiritual life that is so absent from the spirituality
of modern day Western civilization. Yes, we acknowledge the
sacredness of sex but it seems to me that it is a simple and
hypocritical "nod" rather than an embrace of adoring love. We
have lost the understanding that God can possess. Instead we
consider possession by the divine at best as something limited to
cloistered mystics and more likely, at its usual and worst, demonic
or a sure sign of mental illness.

The Old Testament is replete with the story of the
Israelites' eradication of the Canaanites, the native people who
inhabited the "Promised Land," and whose worship was similar
to that of the Sumerians. Time and again the biblical prophets
condemned their sexual practices as they worshipped, on the hill
tops, Astarte and Baal, the goddess and god of fertility. The hill top
is an allusion to high places, such as the ziggurat recounted above,
where sexual worship was offered.

Even today the voice of the prophets of Jehovah, the
God of the Jews, rings consistently in our ears, condemning in the
harshest terms those who would deviate from the sexual mores and
morals of Puritan New England or the homophobic and anti-sexual
teachings of the celibates in the Vatican.

India

Like that of Sumer, the spirituality of the sub-continent of India is difficult for us to understand, even if the twentieth century did see a noticeable influx of Hindu, Taoist and Buddhist thought and practices into our American landscape. The modern-day popularity of meditative and yogic practices certainly illustrates our receptivity to Indian religions but that hardly means we grasp them.

I have to admit to my own confusion in this matter. Having a decidedly linear viewpoint of history, it was natural for me to think of the religions and philosophies of the East as distinct. When Tantric practices came to my attention, my confusion only increased, as it did even further when I learned that Taoism varied from both Hinduism and Buddhism. I wanted to categorize each view in its own neat box with a "founding prophet" and a date and place for the revelation of each. Alas, my Western mind cannot do so. Yoga, for instance, is neither a religion nor a philosophy as we in the West understand those terms. In fact the word yoga simply means yoke, implying the tying together of two parts that are not often united.

Therein lies the critical difference. Whereas Christianity's understanding of the world is based upon faith, Buddhism is based on experiences that proceed from events that one practices, such as meditation, the physical exercises of yoga, and the control of one's breathing.

As you can see in the following quotes, Aurobindo (a reknowned author) describes the difference in approaches, namely that the primary comprehension of the "highest Truth" in the East is by experience.

> In the East, especially in India, the
> metaphysical thinkers have tried, as in the West,
> to determine the nature of the highest Truth by the

intellect. But, in the first place, they have not given mental thinking the supreme rank as an instrument in the discovery of Truth, but only a secondary status. The first rank has always been given to spiritual intuition and illumination and spiritual experience; an intellectual conclusion that contradicts this Supreme authority is held invalid. Secondly, each philosophy has armed itself with a practical way of reaching to the supreme state of consciousness, so that even when one begins with Thought, the aim is to arrive at a consciousness beyond mental thinking. Each philosophical founder (as also those who continued his work or school) has been a metaphysical thinker doubled with a Yogi. Those who were only philosophic intellectuals were respected for their learning, but never took rank as truth-discoverers. And the philosophies that lacked a sufficiently powerful means of spiritual experience died out and became things of the past, because they were not dynamic for spiritual discovery and realization.[6]

In the West it was just the opposite that came to pass. Thought, intellect, the logical reason came to be regarded more and more as the highest means and even the highest end; in philosophy, Thought is the be-all and the end-all. It is by intellectual thinking and speculation that the truth is to be discovered; even spiritual experience has been summoned to pass the tests of the intellect, if it is to be held valid -- just the reverse of the Indian position. Even those who see that mental Thought must be over-passed and admit a supramental "Other", do not seem to escape from the feeling that it must be through mental Thought, sublimating and transmuting itself, that this other Truth must be reached and made to take the place of the mental limitation and ignorance. And, again, Western thought has ceased to be dynamic; it has sought after a theory of things, not after realization.[7]

37

The idea of polytheism is anathema, to say the least, to the Judeo-Christian worldview. We cannot easily imagine the myriad of gods, goddesses, entities, and demons that fill the Indian mind. Bathing in the Ganges, cremation in funeral pyres, temples adorned with the most graphic, imaginative, and often grotesque figures stand in stark contrast to the "proper" religion of middle class America. Chants, mantras, gurus, holy men, a caste system, reincarnation, and many more ideas are often completely foreign to our sensibilities. If that is not enough, the difficulty in understanding the vocabulary of Hinduism is itself a challenge.

As author Alan Watts makes clear in several of his books on Eastern philosophy, even those concepts that have been translated into English were often translated by English linguists who had little understanding of the spiritual concepts that underlay the Indian vocabulary. Still we need to make an attempt at understanding if we are to increase our awareness of the life of the divine.

The oldest writings of what is now Hinduism are found in ancient texts called Vedas:

> The Vedas are the ancient scriptures or revelation (Shruti) of the Hindu teachings. They manifest the Divine Word in human speech. They reflect into human language the language of the Gods, the Divine powers that have created us and which rule over us.
> There are four Vedas, each consisting of four parts. The primary portion is the mantra or hymn section (samhita). To this are appended ritualistic teachings (brahmana) and theological sections (aranyaka). Finally philosophical sections (Upanishads) are included. The hymn sections are the oldest. The others were added at a later date and each explains some aspect of the hymns or follows one line of interpreting them.
> The Vedas were compiled around the time

of Krishna (c. 3500 B.C.), and even at that time were hardly understood. Hence they are very ancient and only in recent times has their spiritual import, like that of the other mystery teachings of the ancient world, begun to be rediscovered or appreciated even in India. Like the Egyptian teachings they are veiled, symbolic and subtle and require a special vision to understand and use properly.

The great compiler of the Veda and Puranas was Vyasa Krishna Dwaipayana. He was said to be the twenty-eighth of the Vyasas or compilers of Vedic knowledge. He was somewhat older than the Avatar Krishna and his work continued after the death of Krishna. Perhaps he is symbolic of a whole Vedic school which flourished at that time, as many such Vedic schools were once prominent all over India and in some places beyond.[8]

When we look beyond the style of their worship and the multiplicity of gods they seem to adore, there is a resident power in the depth of their meditation. Indeed much of the presentation on energy in chapter four, "The Power Exchange," was gleamed from their wisdom.

Hindus seek God within by stilling their minds and clearing it of all entrapments. Their traditions are as ancient as that of the Sumerians, even if the version that we have of their most notable book is more recent.

The Bhagavad-Gita is contained in book six of the great Hindu epic, Mahabharata, probably the longest poem in all of literature. The Gita was written between the fifth century BC and the second century CE and is attributed to Vyasa. According to [the twentieth century guru] Aurobindo [1872-1950], who studied Vyasa's writings, nothing disproves his authorship. The Mahabharata tells the story of a civil war in ancient India between the sons of Kuru (Kauruvas) and the sons of Pandu (Pandavas) over a kingdom the Pandavas believe was stolen from them by the cheating of the Kauruvas. Every attempt by the Pandava brothers to regain their kingdom without war has failed. The Bhagavad Gita is primarily a dialog between Arjuna, the third Pandava brother, and his charioteer, Krishna.[9]

It was Vyasa's genius to take the whole great Mahabharata epic and see it as metaphor for the perennial war between the forces of light and the forces of darkness in every human heart. Arjuna and Krishna are then no longer merely characters in a literary masterpiece. Arjuna becomes Everyman, asking the Lord himself, Sri Krishna, the perennial questions about life and death -- not as a philosopher but as the quintessential man of action. Thus read, the Gita is not an external dialogue but an internal one: between the ordinary human personality, full of questions about the meaning of life, and our deepest Self, which is divine.

There is, in fact, no other way to read the Gita and grasp it as spiritual instruction. If I could offer only one key to understanding this divine dialogue, it would be to remember that it takes place in the depths of consciousness and that Krishna is not some external being, human or superhuman, but the spark of divinity that lies at the core of the human personality. This is not literary or philosophical conjecture; Krishna says as much to Arjuna over and over. "I am the true Self in the heart of every creature, Arjuna, and the beginning, middle, and end of their existence." [10]

On the other hand, author Alan Watts offers a contrary opinion:

The Gita, the discourse on the battlefield between Krishna and the warrior Arjuna, is regarded quite rightly as an epitome of the most profound Hindu doctrines. Yet one of its main points is that

there is no necessary inconsistency between being
a warrior and a yogi, between using the sword and
following the way of spiritual liberation. Today it is,
of course, explained that the battlefield of the Gita is
in fact the human mind, and that the enemies whom
Arjuna is to slay are simply our own passions and evil
propensities. But if that be the case; why does not the
Gita say so? There is nothing so esoteric about this
admonition that it needs to be veiled in symbolism.[11]

Though we often consider Hinduism a polytheistic
religion, Eknath Easwaran, translator of the text of The Bhagavad
Gita I am quoting, makes a good argument to the contrary.
Certainly the teachings of the Vedas and the practice of Hindu
spiritual exercises are meant to bring the devotee to an awareness
of the unity of Reality.

Hinduism has proclaimed one God while
accommodating worship of him (or her, for to millions
God is the Divine Mother) in many different names.
"Truth is one," says a famous verse of the Rig Veda;
"people call it by various names." A monastic devotee
might find that Shiva embodies the austere detachment
he seeks; a devotee who wants to live "in the world,"
partaking of its innocent pleasures but devoted to
service of her fellow creatures, might find in Krishna
the perfect incarnation of her ideals. In every case, this
clothing of the Infinite in human form serves to focus
a devotee's love and to provide an inspiring ideal. But
whatever form is worshiped, it is only an aspect of the
same one God.[12]

These ancient sages were actually exploring
the mind. In profound meditation, they found that
when consciousness is so acutely focused that it
is utterly withdrawn from the body and mind it
enters a kind of singularity in which the sense of a
separate ego disappears. In this state, the supreme
climax of meditation, the seers discovered a core of

consciousness beyond time and change. They called it simply Atman, the Self.[13]

In the teaching of Hinduism, we find early reference to the elements, to energy work, to balance, to holism and ultimate unity, and to the meaning of life. As Sri Krishna says to Arjuna in *The Bhagavad Gita*:

> The body is called a field, Arjuna; he who knows it is called the Knower of the field. This is the knowledge of those who know. I am the Knower of the field in everyone, Arjuna. Knowledge of the field and its Knower is true knowledge.
>
> Listen and I will explain the nature of the field and how change takes place within it. I will also describe the Knower of the field and his power. These truths have been sung by great sages in a variety of ways, and expounded in precise arguments concerning Brahman.
>
> The field, Arjuna, is made up of the following: the five areas of sense perception; the five elements; the five sense organs and the five organs of action; the three components of the mind: manas, buddhi, and ahamkara; and the undifferentiated energy from which all these evolved. In this field arise desire and aversion, pleasure and pain, the body, intelligence, and will.[14]

> That which is the general characteristic of the Indian systems, and that which constitutes their real profundity, is the paramount importance attached to Consciousness and its states. It is these states which create, sustain and destroy the worlds. Brahma, Visnu and Siva are the names for functions of the one Universal Consciousness operating in ourselves. And whatever be the means employed, it is the transformation of the "lower" into "higher" states of consciousness which is the process and fruit of Yoga

and the cause of all its experiences. In this and other
matters, however, we must distinguish both practice
and experience from theory. A similar experience
may possibly be gained by various modes of practice,
and an experience may be in fact a true one, though
the theory which may be given to account for it is
incorrect.[15]

In this last quote, "A similar experience may possibly
be gained by various modes of practice," we have a rare insight
into the spiritual possibilities of BDSM, given to us from a
non-practitioner. It is my conclusion, of course, that both sexual
activity and the kink we so enjoy are a natural pathway to spiritual
experience and that experience can be enhanced by bringing one's
understanding of Spirit into the dungeon and the bedroom.

Ancient Greece

If Western Civilization owes a debt to Judaism and
Christianity, that is not to say that it isn't also the direct descendant
of the glory that was ancient Greece. No study of man and his
relationship to spirit can be complete without reference to the
philosophers of the city-states of the Aegean peninsula.

In Grecian thought can be found the most basic
arguments, propositions, and rationales for Being known to
mankind as well as the basis of our sciences and theologies. They
perfected the use of logic in their arguments, created educational
facilities of renown, and left us a rich legacy of myth, art, epic, and
thought. Socrates, Plato, and Aristotle are only three of a host of
great thinkers who have left us an incomparable legacy.

Still, their world-view was significantly different from
ours, steeped as it was in the legends of gods and goddesses, a
cyclical world destined to repeat itself for all eternity.

A little later, Parmenides of Elea (on the

southwest coast of Italy), claiming Heraclitus had got it exactly backward, asserted that of course the universe had to be stable and permanent-- otherwise it would make no sense at all--and that the constant changes we experience are only accidents, that is, appearances. Our faulty senses misperceive the true nature of things because we have no direct access to ultimate and unchangeable reality. For Heraclitus, change was the only true reality; for Parmenides, it was immutable permanence. Parmenides' long-lasting teacher, the Ionian Xenophanes of Colophon, who lived to be about a hundred and ten, though he made no contribution to these philosophical dialogues about substance and accidents, attacked belief in a multiplicity of gods, as well as Homer's presentation of the gods as having human faults and passions. God was one, said Xenophanes, eternal, effecting things by mind alone and bearing no resemblance whatsoever to flip-flopping mankind. On another front entirely, his observations of sea-shells in the mountains and fossil fish in the quarries of Syracuse convinced Xenophanes that the earth had once been covered in water and would be so again--since, as the Greeks assumed, reality was like a great wheel and all things return. What has been will be again.[16]

A group of fifth-century [B.C.E.] philosophers, headed by Empedocles of Acragas in [the Greek colony of] Sicily, returned to the pursuit of the eternal substance and proposed that there were actually four basic elements out of which everything is composed in varying proportions. These elements are earth, air, fire, and water--a system of categories that science, medicine, and psychology would continue to rely on right into the early modern period.[17]

One of the more notable contributions of ancient Greece to my understanding of sex and spirituality rests in the myths of two of Zeus' sons: Apollo and Dionysos. One is hard pressed to find any two brothers less alike than this pair, reflecting the duality that is the hallmark of Greek thought, a duality that permeates our contemporary understanding of good and evil and spirit and flesh.

Friedrich Nietzsche (1844-1900) is credited as the Father of the "Death of God" philosophy and erroneously condemned by many believers as an atheist. His earth-shattering and theology-rendering writings reverberate even today, more than 100 years after his death. As Thomas Cahill notes in *Sailing the Wine-Dark Sea*, his book on Greece's contribution to Western civilization:

> [It] is not necessary to buy Nietzsche's whole thesis in order to find his categories useful. Apollo, giver of sunlight and measurement, the great archer whose arrows never miss their targets, is the god of severe justice, the god in whom the sense of order is paramount, the one who cannot rest till all wrongs have been righted and all corners have been plumbed. It is Apollo who cannot bear to allow Oedipus to continue his reign and whose holy and uncanny presence is felt throughout Sophocles's play, sparking supernatural fear in all who sense his proximity. The divine model for the typical human hero, Apollo stands in stark contrast to Dionysos, dark lord from the East, giver of the vine, showing himself an alluringly effeminate youth with long, luxuriant hair, surrounded by the vines that entangle others and attended by his satyrs--boisterous creatures from the countryside, horned, betailed, goat-footed (the very images that would be adopted by Christian artists to portray devils), enormous penises erect, subhuman sex machines always at the ready. This was the god for whom the Dionysia was celebrated, whose primitive choruses--called tragodiai (goat-songs)--were the origin of drama. Even in fifth-century Athens, the trilogies of the great tragedians each ended with a short satyr (or satyric) play, a coarse burlesque of mythic material connected to the preceding trilogy.

It helped to set aside all that tragic seriousness and brought the day to a merry close, introducing the night of drinking that lay ahead.

That the Greeks consecrated so much time to such a god suggests they had some inkling of the dark forces that could conquer their best strivings, their quest for arete, and they meant to pay these forces sufficient homage to keep them at bay. The lost utopias of cloud-bound Ithaca and lofty Troy had been replaced by a real-life ideal, a polis of visionary perfection, democratic Athens and its many imitators, a system in which all the inevitable political tensions were kept in balance by "agreements that profit no one to violate." The symposium and the Dionysia were two of several characteristically Greek safety valves for blowing off the social steam that might otherwise build to an explosion. But the libations, the choruses, and the processions were also pleas to the gods to leave their ideal polis intact, not visit it with the ills that had destroyed so many others.[18]

Unlike the calmly balanced Apollo, Dionysos precipitates growth and change, rather than ruling over sameness and stasis.[19]

It is exactly this duality that plays out in our kinky sex. We can easily see ourselves as Dionysians in an Apollonian civilization. More particularly our Dominant/submissive (D/s) relationships, highly structured as they are, reflect the order of Apollo, as does the carefulness of our techniques. We are Dionysian in our quest for ecstasy, for the personal insight and revelation that comes during the bliss of subspace and the abandonment of self to the pain of the whip.

Lest we consider Dionysos as a minor god in a Greek pantheon of many, whose only claim to fame (as if that wasn't enough) was the drunken orgies of Bacchanalia, Dionysian author

Walter Otto writes:

> All of antiquity extolled Dionysos as the
> god who gave man wine. However, he was known
> also as the raving god whose presence makes man
> mad and incites him to savagery and even to lust for
> blood. He was the confidant and companion of the
> spirits of the dead. Mysterious dedications called him
> the Lord of Souls. To his worship belonged the drama
> which has enriched the world with a miracle of the
> spirit. The flowers of spring bore witness to him, too.
> The ivy, the pine, the fig tree were dear to him. Yet
> far above all of these blessings in the natural world of
> vegetation stood the gift of the vine, which has been
> blessed a thousand fold. Dionysos was the god of the
> most blessed ecstasy and the most enraptured love.
> But he was also the persecuted god, the suffering and
> dying god, and all whom he loved, all who attended
> him, had to share his tragic fate.[20]

It is both of these Dionysian elements that we celebrate
in our dungeons. Foremost, of course, is the attention we pay to
ecstasy, which in our subculture we call "subspace," that blissful
event that is the goal of our sadomasochistic play. To fly when
bound, to experience joy while being flogged, to arouse one
another into heightened orgasm is much of what we are about. Still
our play is sadistic and masochistic, celebrating the Dionysian
aspects of suffering and dying, reveling in the lash of the whip and
the blood sport of needles and knives. Murals revealed in the ruins
of Pompey show followers of Dionysos flogging one another -- a
scene repeated at SM conferences, lifestyle dungeons, and the bed-
and playrooms of Leather folk across the country.

China

From the ancient wisdom of the Vedas arose meditation

47

and the practice of yoga, both of which spread from India to China, where flourished both Taoism and Buddhism. Rather than being religions, per se, they are more properly called philosophies, though ones that lead to spiritual experience.

Quoting Alan Watts, again we find ourselves having to confront what seems to be an impossible cultural and linguistic chasm.

> Thus scientific convention decides whether an eel shall be a fish or a snake, and grammatical convention determines what experiences shall be called objects and what shall be called events or actions. How arbitrary such conventions may be can be seen from the question, "What happens to my fist [noun-object] when I open my hand?" The object miraculously vanishes because an action was disguised by a part of speech usually assigned to a thing! In English the differences between things and actions are clearly, if not always logically, distinguished, but a great number of Chinese words do duty for both nouns and verbs so that one who thinks in Chinese has little difficulty in seeing that objects are also events, that our world is a collection of processes rather than entities.[21]

> Zen Buddhism is a way and a view of life which does not belong to any of the formal categories of modern Western thought. It is not religion or philosophy; it is not a psychology or a type of science. It is an example of what is known in India and China as a "way of liberation," and is similar in this respect to Taoism, Vedanta, and Yoga. As will soon be obvious, a way of liberation can have no positive definition. It has to be suggested by saying what it is not, somewhat as a sculptor reveals an image by the act of removing pieces of stone from a block...
> The origins of Zen are as much Taoist as Buddhist, and, because its flavor is so peculiarly

Chinese, it may be best to begin by inquiring into its Chinese ancestry -- illustrating, at the same time, what is meant by a way of liberation by the example of Taoism.[22]

Foremost in the understanding of both Taoism and Zen is the fact that they are primarily practical paths. It is through practice, rather than faith or doctrine, that one finds the truth. Whereas Christianity proclaims first repentance and then salvation that leads to right living, the Chinese view is that the doing, or the not-doing as one might call it, of meditation or yoga, leads to experiential understanding. Whereas we see the contemplative state as the earthly fulfillment of the Christian message, in the East its practice is the beginning of wisdom.

Taoism, Confucianism, and Zen are expressions of a mentality which feels completely at home in this universe, and which sees man as an integral part of his environment. Human intelligence is not an imprisoned spirit from afar but an aspect of the whole intricately balanced organism of the natural world, whose principles were first explored in the Book of Changes. Heaven and earth are alike members of this organism, and nature is as much our father as our mother, since the Tao by which it works is originally manifested in the yang and the yin -- the male and female, positive and negative principles which, in dynamic balance, maintain the order of the world. The insight which lies at the root of Far Eastern culture is that opposites are relational and so fundamentally harmonious. Conflict is always comparatively superficial, for there can be no ultimate conflict when the pairs of opposites are mutually interdependent. Thus our stark divisions of spirit and nature, subject and object, good and evil, artist and medium are quite foreign to this culture.[23]

49

It is this view of the essential unity of Reality that permeates the beliefs of the East, as contrasted with the Western paradigm which is based on duality. Both Indian and Chinese philosophy see first unity from which springs duality, whereas we base many of our perceptions on duality, quickly differentiating, for instance, right from wrong, good from evil, and God from Satan. It is just this rush to dualism that posits that flesh, and therefore sex, is evil, since our dualistic approach must separate spirit and flesh.

Israel

It was Abraham, the progenitor of the Israelites, and his descendants who first arrived at the linear view of history that so fully colors our Western perspective. As historian Tom Cahill explains:

> For the ancients, the future was always to be a replay of the past, as the past was simply an earthly replay of the drama of the heavens: "History repeats itself" -- that is, false history, the history that is not history but myth. For the Jews, history will be no less replete with moral lessons. But the moral is not that history repeats itself but that it is always something new: a process unfolding through time, whose direction and end we cannot know, except insofar as God gives us some hint of what is to come. The future will not be what has happened before; indeed, the only reality that the future has is that it has not happened yet. It is unknowable; and what it will be cannot be discovered by auguries -- by reading the stars or examining entrails. We do not control the future because it is the collective responsibility of those who are bringing about the future by their actions in the present. For this reason, the concept of future -- for

the first time -- holds out promise, rather than just the same old thing. We are not doomed, not bound to some predetermined fate; we are free. If anything can happen, we are truly liberated -- as liberated as were the Israelite slaves when they crossed the Red Sea of Reeds.[24]

In addition to this linear view of history, one of the more profound influences of Judaism on Western civilization was the introduction, through Christianity, of monotheism. Though the descendants of Abraham did not have a complete monopoly on the concept of there being one God, it was central to their concept of divinity and thus was a position unique among the world religions of pre-Christian societies. With the gradual demise of paganism after the Christianization of the Roman Empire under Constantine, monotheism became foundational in Western thought and practice.

As noted, Eastern religious practices, though replete with the worship of many gods, also held to a belief in the oneness of divinity. Though they expressed the Divine in a myriad of names and aspects, there is strong evidence that they believed, at least among the more educated practitioners, God to be One. It is this understanding of Reality that is at the heart of Buddhism and Hinduism.

As Arthur Avalon writes:

> The Devata I worship is the Devata whom the world worships. I do not think of Siva, Sakti, Surya, Ganesa, Visnu, or whomsoever else you may mention, as nothing to me, and as one whom I cannot worship, for all of them are but different aspects, assumed in play, of Him whom I do worship.[25]

In any case -- and here we could go on forever about the

theological differences -- the basic idea of Unity is fundamental to a functional understanding of the relationship of all things to all things and certainly of sex to spirit. It is our condition as members of the culture of the West that we see life in all its manifestations within a context of duality. "Hear, O Israel: The Lord our God is one Lord"[26] is the foundation, then, of our theology but is quickly trumped by the belief that God is Other than us, thereby creating in our minds a duality.

Jehovah, the Lord God of the Old Testament, is easily seen as a jealous and demanding God throughout the history of Jewish people. There could be no other gods before him and those who worshipped other gods were to be annihilated. Instead of promoting the tolerance that polytheism necessitated, monotheism promoted a rigidly exclusive view of the world, a theological us-versus-them division.

It can be easily seen that part of this was necessitated by the desire of the Hebrews (or at least their leadership) to mold Israel into a sovereign nation, since the union of church and state has almost always and everywhere been a foregone conclusion in the world of politics. Separation of church and state is, in comparison, a rather new idea historically. Our Western understanding of freedom of religion was totally foreign to the citizens of nations of the past. Church and state were one in the eyes of the ancients, even to the degree that the rulers were not only God-ordained but often were gods themselves, as we have seen with Gilgamesh in Sumer and in the divinity of the pharaohs of Egypt. The Hebrews, then, were inspired to conquer and eradicate the Canaanites who were dwelling in the land that was promised to them, for there could only be one theocracy if a country were to be a nation -- a conflict that still rages to this day in the Middle East.

Canaan (also called Phoenicia) was a land

of ancient Semitic peoples which included most of the area that makes up modern Israel and Syria. Like its West Asian neighbors it was made up of city-states (Tyre, Sidon, Ugarit and Byblos) which traded with all the larger empires around them. In fact the Canaanites or Phoenicians were talented sailors who spread far and wide, connecting disparate cultures through trade as well as transmitting their own ideas. They were eventually taken over by other powers in that ever-changing area of migration and conflict, and being of the same Semitic racial stock they were absorbed by Hebrew culture.

The Canaanite polytheistic religion contained a large pantheon, headed by the gods El and Baal and goddesses Asherah and Astarte. The emphasis was on fertility, reflecting the importance of water for agriculture in that dry region. Deities were sacrificed to in high places and at temples and shrines in ways similar to Israel and other Semitic cultures.

The Hebrews shifted and shunted through war and conquest, melding the ideas of the moment and those of the great civilizations around them. They emerged from the nexus of a dynamic and changing world to form through ordeal and trial the master plan of their religion -- which would penetrate geographical distance and time to become, along with its similarly-sourced cousin, Islam, one of the two most dominant religions of the modern world. For the Hebrews perfected the West Asian tendency toward monotheism. El and Yaweh had similarities that were eventually curtailed, both gods were detached and omnipotent, hiding a jealous and competitive sensitivity. Yaweh evolved perhaps from various city gods including Sin, the chief deity of Abraham's home city of Ur, and Akhenaten's Aten about whom Moses would have heard. At this time people were seriously mixing and exchanging data and theory. The Hebrew creator god even told Jonah that the Hebrews held no exclusive rights to him -- he was a worldwide

god whose message was for all humankind. There
were to be no others, no images and therefore little
mythology.[27]

Because the Lord God of the Jews demanded that there
would be no other gods before Him, the eradication of the high
places of the Canaanites and hence their worship of false gods was
a foregone conclusion. Since theirs was a fertility religion, sexual
worship, abhorred by the Hebrew God, was forbidden. These are
the same Old Testament prohibitions that inspire sex-negativity in
our modern society.

Rather than seeing prohibitions against homosexuality
and temple prostitution as religious events and therefore forbidden,
Christian exegesis extrapolates extra-marital (and at times even
non-procreative) sex as evil. A truer reading of the Old Testament
prohibitions reveals that it is speaking against non-Hebrew
religious practices rather than purely sexual practices. That said,
one can conclude, as I am doing in this book, that all sexual
activity is indeed spiritual activity. Hence the prohibitions can be
seen to have force within that context, if one wishes to be either a
fully observant Jew or a fundamentalist Christian. I will leave that
discussion to Rabbinical and Christian theologians.

The Romans

Closer to home, so to speak, we need to explore the
mystery schools of ancient Rome, though that is not to say that the
ancient world as well as every era since then hasn't had its own
such secret cults and practices.

They had a pantheon of gods, patron-
protectors of various families and tribes...[28]

There were, however, many alternatives,
not a few of them shadowy and fugitive. These were

called "the Mysteries" (from the Greek mystes, an
initiate, and mysteria, the rites of initiation). The
Mysteries were secret cults into which one had to be
initiated -- and they have kept their secrets. To this
day, we have little more than informed speculation as
to what the majority of them entailed.[29]

It is in the practice of initiation, "the rites, ceremonies,
ordeals, or instructions with which one is made a member of a
sect, or society or is invested with a particular function or status,"
that we might well see the closest parallel between the spiritual
quests of the ancient world and the scenes of twenty-first century
American Leather. One might even surmise that it is the decline
of initiatory practices in modern America that has given rise to the
popularity of BDSM. Having given up the acknowledgement of
passages in life through initiatory rituals, we are re-creating them
in our BDSM groups.

Though there is little record of what transpired in these
mystery schools, anthropologists have recorded ample practices
among "primitive" societies in the last century and half. We
are now seeing the adoption of some of these practices into
our fetish play, such as energy pulls and bell dancing. Here we
have a strong deviation from the usual intellectual approach to
Spirit. The piercing, cuttings, and masochistic pain are meant to
lead to ecstasy and therefore revelation, not unlike what we can
extrapolate from the fragments which speak of the initiations of
ancient Greek and Rome, to mention only two of the many.

A fragment of Aristotle preserved in
Synesius (Dio 10) provides the occasion for a
final word on the ancient mystery religions. In this
fragment Aristotle concludes that initiates into the
mysteries do not learn anything (ou mathein ti), but
rather have an experience (pathein) and are put in a
certain state of mind (diatethenal). There is much to

commend this conclusion. While the ancient initiates may have been emotionally affected by the rituals and may have gained insight into divine profundities through the legomena, deiknymena, and dromena, they were not given instruction or taught doctrine in any traditional sense. Initiation was not classroom education, but an eye-opening experience that transcended earthly realities and mundane learning. Just as any mystical experience ultimately cannot be put into words or described adequately in books, so also the blessed mystai heard, saw, and performed the ineffable. They claimed to have tasted death and life and to have been touched by the divine. United with one or another of the deities of the mystery religions -- including, some scholars would say, Christ -- they beheld the light, and their lives were renewed.[30]

Culture & BDSM

Just as we can discuss the cultures of twenty-first century America, ancient Rome, or Europe of the Middle Ages, so too can we consider that kinky folk have a culture, or more properly, a sub-culture of their own. As a sub-culture it represents a minority (and a small one at that) of the population. Not only is it sub-cultural but in many ways, as I have said before, it is counter-cultural and hence is subject to negative actions on the part of the primary cultural forces. This is reflected, needless to say, in laws against public sex and nudity, in prosecution by state and federal government of those who produce BDSM videos, and even in the difficulty of holding public events in hotels and convention halls.

The mere pervasiveness of the primary culture enforces a sense that it is normative, thereby automatically implying that our contrary sub-culture is not. It is this attitude that engenders either low or negative self-esteem in BDSM practitioners as practitioners. It is easier to agree with the majority than to assert one's right to self-determination in one's sexual practice.

Considering other cultures allows us to gain a better understanding of what is normal and to recognize that one culture, even if it is primary, is not necessarily better, wiser, or more conducive to happiness than another. Indeed, reflecting on the fertility rites of Sumer or the cultural war between Israel and Canaan can give us significant insight into the cultural battles that we SM practitioners must face.

Additionally such consideration gives us a different perspective from which to analyze and understand what we do. For instance Gay men have long used the euphemism "cock worship" to describe oral-genital sex. When we reflect on the phallic rites of ancient civilizations we can conclude that for some cock worship is more than just a euphemism and may in fact have an explicit and legitimate role in religious practice, much to the chagrin of the primary culture.

To understand that fertility rites may have involved the springtime ejaculating of semen into the fields in order to ensure a bountiful harvest is to call into serious question the prohibitions against masturbation. Acknowledging that temple-based sexual intercourse was, for many, a religious rite is to remove it from the realm of prostitution and restore it to its rightful place as a theologically sound and even necessary activity.

What many in the primary culture condemn as lascivious, shameful, and evil can now be seen as beneficial, beautiful, and of a spiritual good.

I hope this then gives you a fresh starting point in considering spirit in your life. My approach is meant to be two-fold. First it is eclectic, adding bits and pieces to the solution of the puzzle from wherever they may be found. Second, but certainly not subordinate, is to keep all these pieces in some kind of unified, i.e., holistic framework.

It also seems to me that since each of the spiritualities presented thus far was born and nurtured within a specific cultural milieu we would do well to create and nurture that spirituality most attuned to our own nature. We are neither ancient nor primitive, solely intellectual nor experiential. Let us then venture on the path most authentic to our individual psyches and most conducive to bringing both ourselves and our environment (in its broadest sense) to fruition.

Reflecting on Philosophy In the Dungeon

Permeated as our society is by present-day theology, especially those relating to Judaism, Christianity, and to a lesser degree Islam, Buddhism, and Hinduism, we have little more than a historical or anthropological sense of other belief systems. Even when we consider them we rate them as pagan or primitive, thereby making them diminutive and degraded. We subconsciously assert that a larger number of believers must mean that one faith is "better" than another, that Judaism, for instance, is superior to the worship of Baal because the Jews conquered the Canaanites or that Christianity is superior to Greco and Roman religion because it "triumphed."

Rather than rate one religion better than another, might not a more eclectic approach be to our advantage? What can Christian chant, as an example, add to Buddhist meditation? Just as Karl Jung looked to ancient mythology to find archetypes for his understanding of psychology, might there not be ideas in the worship found in the temples of Greece that might shed light on the prayer life found in the Sistine Chapel or Westminster Abbey?

While honoring your own tradition, what can other traditions add to your understanding, your faith, and your practice? What from history can you bring into your present to make yourself more whole?

1   I Corinthians 13.9-13, *Harper Study Bible*, Revised Standard Version, Zondervan Publishing House, Inc., 1965.

2   Before Christian Era.

3   Grundy, Stephan, *Gilgamesh*, William Morrow, New York, 2000.

4   *Gilgamesh*, pages 43-44.

5   *Gilgamesh*, page 85.

6   Aurobindo, Sri, *The Riddle of This World,* Sri Aurobindo Ashram, Ponicherry, 1951, pages 27-28.

7   *Gilgamesh*, pages 28-29.

8   From *The Hindu Universe* found at http://www.hindunet.org/vedas/index.htm on December 27, 2005.

9   From the *Wisdom Bible*, published by World Peace Foundation, Goleta, CA, and found at http://www.san.beck.org/Gita.html in December, 2005.

10   Easwaran, Eknath, *The Bhagavad Gita*, Vintage Books, New York, 2000, page xix.

11   Elisofon, Eliot and Watts, Alan, *The Temple of Konarak*, Erotic Spirituality, Thames and Hudson, London, 1971, pages 57-58.

12   *The Bhagavad Gita*, page xx.

13   *The Bhagavad Gita*, page xxiii.

14   *The Bhagavad Gita*, page 69.

15   Woodroffe, Sir John, writing as Arthur Avalon, *Principles of Tantra*, Ganesh & Co., 1978, page 19.

16   Cahill, Thomas, *Sailing the Wine-Dark Sea*, Anchor Books, New York, 2004, page 147.

17   *Sailing the Wine-Dark Sea*, page 148.

18   *Sailing the Wine-Dark Sea*, pages 142-143.

19   *Sailing the Wine-Dark Sea*, page 227.

20   Otto, Walter F., *Dionysus, Myth and Cult*, Spring Publications, Dallas, Texas, 1965, page 49.

21   Watts, Alan W., *The Way of Zen*, Vintage Books, New York, 1957, page 5.

22   *The Way of Zen*, page 3.

23   *The Way of Zen*, page 175.

24   Cahill, Thomas, *The Gifts of the Jews*, Anchor Books, Doubleday, New York, 1998, pages 130-131.

25   *Principles of Tantra*, page 382.

26   Deuteronomy 6:4, *Revised Standard Version*.

27   Forty, Jo, *Mythology, A Visual Encyclopedia*, PRC Publishing Ltd, London, page 54-56.

28   *Sailing the Wine-Dark Sea*, page 252.

29   *The Gifts of the Jews*, page 254.

30   Meyer, Marvin W., Editor, *The Ancient Mysteries, A Sourcebook*, Harper & Row, San Francisco, 1987, pages 12-13.

Chapter

The Power Exhange **4**

Brain waves as detected by scientists reflect movement, a form of energy. Endorphins, being compounds composed of chemicals, are a form of matter. Here in the West we have long considered that energy and matter are a duality, separate and unique. That perspective, of course, was greatly altered by Albert Einstein's famous equation that "$E=mc^2$."[1]

Although I passed my classes in Physics I'm not about to try and shed much light on his formula. Simply put it means that energy and mass are interrelated, even interchangeable. A good example of this is the transformation of sunlight by a leaf into sugar, with the assist of chlorophyll and the necessary nutrients. Likewise our bodies use matter (sugar) to create energy as demonstrated in the movement of our muscles.

In Eastern cultures there is a fundamental understanding that all existence is a manifestation of energy. Buddhists believe that all things, humans included, are forces of energy and have arrived at an understanding of human existence based on such a premise.

Before I continue this chapter, though, I'll need to remind you that I'm neither a Tibetan monk nor a Hindu guru. Oh, I've done my stint of studying at a New Age center and have read more self-help books on visualization, karma, and inner work than most guys raised in an Italian-American family, but don't think that my short explanation will suffice for ten years of study in a Himalayan monastery. That disclaimer noted, allow me to spout off on one of my favorite subjects: our energetic bodies.

My first encounter with the subject came in late 1983 from a friend named Ronn who suggested that I might benefit from what he called an energy balancing. At the time I had no idea what he meant. He simply told me to lie on my back on a blanket on the floor with my hands at my side and to relax. He put some New Age music on the stereo. I closed my eyes and he quietly and slowly moved his hands slightly above my body.

I later learned that he was giving me an "energy balancing," the end result of which put me in a calm and pleasant state of relaxation. Eventually, of course, Ronn explained to me the theory and practice of what he was doing. His teacher, Conrad, had learned the process, at least in part, from a man named Brugh Joy, MD. The story of how Dr. Joy learned the process is found in his book, *Joy's Way*², which I highly recommend to anyone who wants to learn more about themselves and the energetic world in which we live.

Simply put, Joy presents an experiential and medical view of what Eastern cultures call the chakras, centers of energy that sustain, create, and influence the human body. Various gurus have different understandings and they all vary in the details of their explanations. Following Joy's understanding of Eastern physiology, there are eight primary chakras: the root, the sexual center, the solar plexus, the heart, the throat, the third eye, the crown, and the transpersonal point. (See illustration two.)

Each chakra is assigned different attributes and functions and is a "center" of energy. An energy balancing, then, is meant to equalize the energy in each chakra in order to bring them into harmonic balance. What Ronn had noticed about me was that my energy centers were "blocked," out of balance, and hence out of harmony. I'm not sure how he knew that as I certainly didn't feel that way, but I have to admit that after his ministrations I felt lighter, more peaceful, and certainly more balanced and grounded.

The only negative effect in what he did was that occasionally I would feel a spasm of energy "sparking" from one part of my body to another. It would cause me to jerk uncontrollably, with a bit of shock, but certainly nothing very painful or long-lasting. Ronn explained that this was simply energy moving into equilibrium, a sign that my chakras were becoming more balanced.

As I said, Joy's book goes into much more detail about this process and gives actual techniques that one can use on oneself or one's partner. In short, Joy suggests that one start with the heart chakra, letting it open by a process of intention and visualization (more on this later). One then visualizes the heart energy connecting to other chakras one by one in a circular path: heart to throat, throat to solar plexus, solar plexus to third eye, third eye to sexual center, sexual center to crown, crown to root, and root to transpersonal point. (See illustration two.)

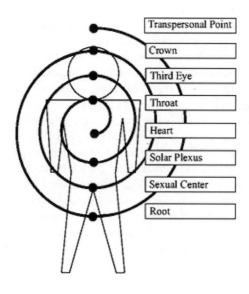

Illustration Two.

The placement of the eight primary chakras according to Brugh Joy. The spiral, beginning at the heart and flowing to the transpersonal point, illustrates the path encouraged by Joy's Energy Balancing.

Each center, as I said, has its own attributes, color, vibration, realm of influence, etc., depending upon the teaching of the individual guru. As I wrote in *Partners in Power*, Brugh characterizes them this way:

> Each of these chakras has associated with it various characteristics. The root is our connection with the earth. Through it we bond with all of physical creation, with Mother Earth, the sustaining and nourishing goddess. The root allows us to ground ourselves and experience stability. It is also our connection through which we can both draw enormous energy and allow excess energy to drain. Electrical engineers have long taught that the earth is, after all, a boundless source for grounding.
>
> The sexual center, which some teachers consider one with the root, is the seat of sexual energy. It is from here that Tantric adepts teach that the coiled serpent, the Kundalini [more on this later] energy, arises from the groin, spirals up the torso, and brings enlightenment. The solar plexus is the center associated with fear and gut instinct, hence the idea that we have "butterflies" in our bellies and feel anxious in the pit of our stomach. Likewise comes the acknowledgment of intestinal fortitude as there is strength of will there as well. Even we Westerners recognize the heart chakra as the center of love energy. The throat chakra is known as the center of creativity and the center of willingness, hence the "lump in my throat." The third eye (forehead area between and above the eyebrows) is the center of understanding and seeing, also known as the inner eye. The crown chakra is the seat of knowing, of ideas, and of thought. The top-most center, the transpersonal point, is one

that is often omitted by many practitioners. It is my experience, taking my cue from Joy, that this center is my connection to divinity, the Sky Father.[4]

Sometime in 1985 I awoke in the middle of the night with intense pain in my stomach. I thought it was appendicitis and I was quite frightened. I dressed and walked the two blocks to the emergency room of the nearest hospital, where I was admitted. Three days later I was released, the pain gone and no specific diagnosis given, except that I had "acute pancreatitis," or pain in my pancreas. At the time I was Director of Religious Education for a large Catholic Publishing Company and one of my consultants, a wonderfully Christian woman and a member of the Sisters of St. Joseph of Carondolet, suggested that my real problem was stress. She urged me to get counseling in stress reduction techniques.

It was then that I began meeting with Ronn's friend and therapist Conrad and my more formal education in meditation and energy work began in earnest.

He advised me to read *Joy's Way* and to attend the various workshops given at his New Age center in Fort Wayne, Indiana. To say that it was a life-changing and enlightening adventure is to put it mildly. Conrad taught me the chakra system and its application in everyday living. Indeed I owe much to his wisdom and training.

Another technique that Conrad taught involved mutual balancing: two partners sit facing one another and in guided imagery imagine their heart chakras opening and sending a beam of light or love to the other. Eventually the partners join their chakras, visualizing a flow of energy between them in various circular paths, a true sharing of one's power, light and love.

A More Eastern Consideration

Dr. Joy's teaching, as found in his writings and presented to me by Conrad, differs from the more traditional teachings of

65

Tibet, India, and China, though the deviations are primarily in form rather than essence. Still, for those who want a more purist approach, it is a good idea to hear an Eastern consideration of power from culturally closer writers.

If you feel drawn to knowing more about Buddhist and Hindu practices, there are a great number of books written about Eastern philosophy, as most gurus consider what they teach to be more a philosophy than a religion. Based on ancient Vedic scriptures, as I note in chapter three, there is a reliance on experience, especially that gained through meditation, and on practices that arouse the energetic centers in a rising to the head and thus godliness followed by the descent of energy back into the body, raising the practitioner to a higher level of spiritual achievement.

This aroused and rising power is called Kundalini, the Coiled Snake. Here is how Gopi Krishna in his book, *A Kundalini Catechism*, describes it::

What is Kundalini?

Kundalini is a divine energy represented by the ancient Indian Masters in the form of a serpent, coiled three and a half times, lying asleep until it is awakened, after which it can, in some cases, bestow super consciousness. Kundalini has been called a goddess, who is guarding a mighty dormant force in the human body, located at the base of the spine. Actually, it is both a force and the controlling mechanism of the force.

What is this force?

As the ancient writers have said, it is the vital force or prana which is spread over both the macrocosm, the entire Universe, and the microcosm, the human body.[5]

In *Gay Soul*, Ed Steinbrecher discusses the same phenomenon:

> Kundalini is a Sanskrit word that defines an energy that sleeps around the tailbone. It translates as "serpent power." It awakens as a side effect of any meditation practice, but very rapidly with the particular meditation I had been doing, and still practice, since 1968. Kundalini, as understood today, is an evolutionary energy. It is pushing us into our next evolutionary step and is awakening now in more and more people. LSD or any of the hallucinogens often awaken spontaneous kundalini experiences. In the West we call it the descent of grace. It requires the union of the masculine and feminine principles.[6]

If your experience is anything like mine, you will find that reading the literature from the East on this subject to be somewhat difficult. Indeed it is felt that an understanding of these principles cannot be effectively taught in a book but that, as I will discuss later, the student must have a guru who will act as mentor, guide, and teacher so that the student can first become aware of these truths experientially. Explanations and descriptions vary from guru to guru as well and there is not a great amount of consistency in either the number, the placement, or the description of the various chakras. Added to these problems is that much of the descriptive language remains in the Sanskrit and is as much allegorical as descriptive. Here for instance is a description of a chakra. I have added (in the brackets) definitions not found in the original quote:

> In the space outside the Meru [spinal column], placed on the left and the right, are the two Siras [Nadis], Sasi [Moon], and Mihira [Sun]. The Nadi Susumna, whose substance is the threefold Gunas, is in the middle. She is the form of Moon,

Sun, and Fire; Her body, a string of blooming Dhatura
flowers, extends from the middle of the Kanda [root
of all the Nadis] to the Head, and the Vajra inside
Her extends, shining, from the Medhra [penis] to the
Head.[7]

In his treatise on Tantra Yoga, Arthur Avalon describes
five chakras, as illustration three depicts: Muladhara, Svadhisthana,
Manipuraka, Anahata, Visuddha, and Ajna. Having done so, he
then adds a sixth (the third eye and combines it with the crown).
See illutration three.

Illustration Three.[8]

The Power Exchange & BDSM

In our Leather subculture, there's a prominent use of the
words Power Exchange, even to the extent that a few groups, such

as the Arizona Power Exchange, have them in their names. If they don't, their members are still rather quick to point out that what we do is exchange power. What does this mean?

Power is the "ability to effect change," made possible by the presence of energy, which I define as the force used to effect that change. Both of these words have a myriad of connotations and we use them quite freely. Examples are found in sentences such as "She has such a power over him" and "There was a really good energy in the dungeon last night."

What we often fail to note when we say these things is that the power of the mind is necessary to effect human change. Seemingly random energy effects change but there is no telling what kind of change. The power exchange in which we engage, then, is directed by will, by consciousness, by intent. For me, this seems to be a fundamental and unalterable part of human existence. In this universe it appears that mind and energy unite to create, even if our creation is destructive. As W. Clement Stone wrote, "Whatever the mind of man can conceive, it can achieve.[8]"

Partners are involved in a "power exchange" in that they agree (the mind part of the event) to combine their power to effect some kind of change. In BDSM this exchange is most often meant to change one's perceptions and feelings, i.e., to move into subspace, to enjoy an orgasm, to experience pleasure, etc. Sometimes it appears that one partner is only receiving power rather than exchanging it but a closer examination reveals that even the receiving partner (the bottom) is using their own energy in some way, such as when their body releases endorphins or other hormones, when they use their muscle power to move or not move, or when they surrender their energy to the power of their top.

Understanding this "give and take" of energy and the use of "mind over matter" increases our ability to accomplish and to enjoy that which we seek to do. Note that the words "mind over matter" do not mean that mind beats or forces matter, as in "The fighter overcomes his opponent." It means that the mind controls and directs the body, as when it sends a message to the bottom's bottom to stop squirming so that the top can hit it without injury.

The top and bottom, then, need to be of one mind, that is, in agreement as to what they are going to do and how it will be done. That's why we negotiate. The union of the energies of both cause the effect, which we call the scene, to be more pleasurable and more effective.

The simple jottings written above aren't always as simple as they sound. Yes, our minds can devise many paths to achieve a goal and sometimes all it takes is a little planning and a little action. At other times, though, even the most in-control minds are stumped and the strongest or most energetic bodies aren't up to the task. That is life on this planet. In those situations we must find additional energetic forces, i.e., ask someone to help us lift this really heavy St. Andrews Cross or ask others to help us devise a plan by giving us their thoughts on the matter.

Too often, unfortunately, it is our own mind that is the obstacle, as when we accept defeat or rush in where angels fear to tread. Mind can achieve but it achieves within the boundaries and limitations, otherwise called the structure, of the universe. Man can fly, not by developing wings (at least not yet), but by building an airplane. The airplane, when you think of it, seems to defy the law of gravity but actually employs the laws of aerodynamics. The Wright brothers had to use their minds to envision flying before they used their machine at Kitty Hawk. In this case, as in most, knowing the rules is what matters.

Our minds, too, sometimes send conflicting directions. This is where poor self-image, negative thinking, and/or lack of perseverance, among others things, conspire to bring us failure. Honestly, though, it is not exactly failure. Rather it is the correct application of the principles of creation. Mind, even when it is thinking negatively, still directs the action, if only subconsciously and in contrariness to what we consciously think we want to accomplish.

Whether it is believing or doubting, happily expecting or horribly dreading, mind directs the way our energy creates. Hence there is the need for balanced, positive, and calm thinking when we wish to create positively. Unpleasant scenes often arise from situations in which we don't understand how the power exchange is working and therefore make assumptions based on that lack of understanding.

At other times we do understand and choose not to heed mind-sent warnings. In this second case, the mind, in a certain sense, gives up its ability to control as we turn the right of directing over to our emotions, our physical being, or another aspect of our existence. As the 1986 song by Romanovsky & Phillips so delightfully reminded Gay men: "Don't Use Your Penis For A Brain."

I hope that all of this makes sense to you. What I fear, though, is that too often we think that metaphysical realities such as this only apply when we are actively creating. We know that artists can be guided by their minds (or whatever you want to call what poets call "The Muses") but fail to take into consideration that the same forces are at work all the time, even when we are not actively conscious of them.

It's not, after all, that we think to make our hearts beat, nor do we have to use our conscious minds to remind us to breathe. Still there is something in "mind" that is working to make certain that we are breathing and our heart is pumping.

Mind

Another problem that needs to be faced is that we often don't understand what constitutes "mind." I know that I don't. It is a very difficult concept to grasp. A Google search on the words "mind definition" returns more than 41 million pages. I looked at the first web page which held more than 30 definitions, and then went on to remind me that we can also look at "conscious mind, subconscious mind, mind mapping, mind map, peace of mind, state of mind, unconscious mind, theory of mind, and a beautiful mind." I like these two (out of ten presented) from Answer.com: "The human consciousness that originates in the brain and is manifested especially in thought, perception, emotion, will, memory, and imagination" and "The collective conscious and unconscious processes in a sentient organism that direct and influence mental and physical behavior."

Yes, those are certainly acceptable definitions, though they don't really shed a great deal of light upon the subject. As noted in the first definition, we Westerners, for example, believe that mind originates in the brain. I know a practitioner of Chinese medicine who explained to me that the body is controlled not by the brain but by the heart. Ancient Egyptian embalmers in preparing bodies for mummification, as another example, drained the brain out of the skull and threw it away. They preferred to save other organs, especially the heart and liver, which to them were the seats of our humanity, not the brain. Once again we find different theories based on different paradigms.

How, then, can we use our brains to enhance our sexual experiences? How can we tap into this "mind control" to direct our energies for pleasure, for creativity, for enhancement of our sexual life, and all of life for that matter?

To begin, it's necessary that we simply acknowledge that our brains are involved. We have to recognize that sex is not a brain-less activity but rather that it is part and parcel of what we do. That's not to say that it's all in our brain. Rather our brain has an important role to play within the context of everything we do, including sex.

Recognition increases our awareness and increased awareness brings the opportunity to learn and grow, to realize that what is happening is within our control and therefore can be enhanced by that control. This is a big realization, as we too often consider that sex is just something done naturally or instinctively. I will agree that there is part instinct in the sex act but good sex is more than just doing what the birds and bees do. It ought to be a holistic endeavor. Therefore the brain ought not to be left out of the doing.

Including the brain in our sexuality activity opens us up to new ways of being sexual. One of those ways is called visualization. For a complete description of this process I encourage you to experiment, and suggest you read a book or two on the subject.[10]

In one sense visualization means that you see in your mind's eye the energy that you are sharing, as I learned from Conrad in his mutual balancing. I do that in a number of ways. For instance, I often "see" a light shining in my heart and send a beam of it out of my chest. I then imagine this beam going from me to my partner, entering his or her chest, and shining upon the heart therein. I may even enhance the visualization by suggesting that they visualize my chest opening, and note the light of my heart shining on and into their heart. I then continue with the suggestion that they do the same, sending the light of their heart to mine. As we share this vision, we share our heart's energy. In another scenario I might send warmth or love.

In a third scenario I might imagine that energy is flowing from my heart, up my chest to my lips and from there, as I am kissing my partner, to their lips and thence down to their heart, returning to mine. The variations are numerous. From the earth to my crotch to my heart, head, and up to the heavens. From the sky, I might see energy falling on my partner and me as a gentle rain. The idea here is that we are bathed, cleansed, and freed by the power that flows between, in, and around us, energizing and lifting both of us into new dimensions of thought, creativity, and peace.

As running water cleanses particles in its path, so can the movement of energy help remove psychic blocks in our lives.

This is no easy and quick process but rather a gentle change of our mindset concerning our fears, angers, hurts, and other negative feelings. It is similar -- though certainly not as dramatic -- as what theater goers call a catharsis. Combined with study, meditation, and a competent counselor, over time we can find ourselves renewed and refreshed, freed from hang-ups that may have paralyzed our sex life, not to mention our lives in general.

The necessary caveat here is that the bedroom is not a proper place for therapy. I am only suggesting that sex can be a liberating activity, given the right partner at the right time.

Stress counselors have noted that sexual activity reduces stress. Certainly the suggestions I am making here can lead to what people who recognize the power exchange call "grounding" or "centering," a process of allowing energy in the form of tension to melt or flow away. Similarly, relaxation techniques can achieve the same result. Indeed much of what I am writing about in these lines is taken from generally accepted advice on how to relax.

In all of this we need to heighten our awareness of the subtle signals we might receive, be they from our partner, our body, or our minds. Too often we disregard that still silent voice, ignoring what may be only a small signal or a slight hint. Ideas, such as to proceed in a certain way, may or may not be helpful, but it is certainly useful to understand that there is value in evaluating them rather than merely disregarding them.

Surrender

Another aspect of good sex is the act of surrender: "To yield to the power, control, or possession of another upon compulsion or demand." The first part of the definition includes both power and control, significant concepts that are the basis of this chapter. On the other hand, compulsion and demand are not part of what it is that we do. So in our context we need to understand surrender as "to willingly yield to the power or control of another." Let me note the obvious. Here we are considering healthy activities between adults who can trust one another in healthy ways.

The best power exchanges, meaning the most enjoyable and the most beneficial, are those between committed and trusting partners. Since surrender indicates a lack of barriers, of blocks, of doubts and fears, one ought not to surrender without these conditions being met.

When one can surrender, on the other hand, there can be intense bonding, a strong sense of belonging, a true freedom to be and to become that which is one's fullest potential. Surrender means that we let go, give up what we fear and doubt. It means that we no longer have expectations of what will or will not occur. It is pointed to in the idea of "letting go." It is primarily an act of faith, an action that shows we believe in a friendly universe where "We know that in all things God works for good with those who love him, who are called according to his purpose,"[11] and that we have faith in the partner to whom we are surrendering. It is also an Eastern philosophy:

> You must trust yourself. You say you
> know yourself too well? If you feel so, you do *not*
> know yourself; you know only the weak outer husk,
> which has fallen often into the mire. But you -- the
> real you -- are a spark of God's own fire, and God,
> who is Almighty, is in you, and because of that there
> is nothing that you cannot do if you will. Say to
> yourself: "What man has done, man can do. I am a
> man, yet also God in man; I can do this thing, and I
> will." For your will must be like tempered steel, if you
> would tread the Path.[12]

Surrender, then, is not a mindless abandon, neither a sense of not caring nor of giving up. Rather it is a state of mind that is open to possibility, believing and expecting to experience that which is good. It does so even in the face of that which we fear and loathe, knowing that there are silver linings in the dark clouds, that good can be realized in every step if we are open to note its presence. This is, after all, about enjoying life in its fullness and sex in particular in the beautiful reality, the real sacredness, that was meant to be experienced.

Induction

Energy is found in many forms. Indeed everything is energy in some form, though we normally consider it to be the "capacity to do work." In the common or colloquial use of the term we often focus more on its manifestation as a sensed phenomenon, such as light, sound, or a vibration. We use the term loosely such as when we say "There was a nice energy in the room last night" or "I felt his energy and he was really down."

Such vagueness in our language communicates but does not communicate well. On the other hand, it is the case that in discussing energy there often just aren't the right words to describe what is happening. Admittedly that may be because we very often don't know what's happening. To that I will add that there are certainly many times when that's the case as far my knowledge goes. I may be writing this book, but I still have lots to learn.

One of the phenomena that is related to energy, and here I mean the energy that is us, is that we often experience it in ways and at times when we are very much unaware that we are doing so. Yes, there are those who are sensitive to the energies that surround them, but for the great majority of us, our brains tune out incoming sensations of many kinds. It would seem that to do so is a matter of necessity, lest we quickly be overwhelmed by a tidal flood of input which, in the final analysis, would make no sense.

Since that is the case, many of the ideas presented in this chapter can be easily dismissed as "hooey" or "crazy" or "unrealistic." As Westerners we certainly have been trained that way. Yet even our language admits to the possibility of such energetic realities, as when we speak of experiences of energy in terms of lightness, bliss, or subspace.

Likewise the energies of others can induce us into a different state of feeling. Some friends always seem to lift us while others, whom we probably don't consider friends, somehow always drag us down. The phenomenon is especially noticeable in the area of emotions, so that in an encounter with an angry person, we're liable to become angry, or else a soft reply to an angry tirade may in fact soothe the one who launched it.

Joy's energy balancing exercise uses induction through the technique of visualization to induce another into a different state. Likewise, our remaining calm, centered, and balanced in a situation may help others to maintain or attain a similar state, just as panic spreads in a negative way. Another way to look at this phenomenon is to consider that associating with successful people tends to make us more successful, while running "with the wrong crowd" will probably get us into trouble.

Any way you look at this, we arrive at the fundamental unity, the "connectedness" of all things, that we are part of a vast, even infinite reality. No matter how far the connections might extend, the link is always, everywhere present. If I drop a stone on the ground, the vibration of its impact continues on, even if there are no devices sensitive enough to detect it.

Balance

The point of this is more than just to teach the important concept of energy, since my purpose is not merely to inform but to lead you to experience. The goal here is to bring each of us into a balanced state, equilibrium, wherein we can find the solid ground of our own being-ness and reside in a strength that cannot be easily shaken.

As long as we are subject to highs and lows, the good days and the bad, we will remain powerless to contemplate reality. It is a call to the middle way, where we can abide between right and left, up and down, good and evil and therefore comprehend clearly. My historical resource Thomas Cahill quotes Archilocus, a sensational athlete and sometime poet of ancient Greece who in his most thoughtful lines seems to

counsel himself in the clear light of day not to excess but to sobriety -- to balance, modesty, and even resignation:

O heart, my heart, no public leaping when you win; no solitude nor weeping when you fail to prove. Rejoice at simple things; and be but vexed by sin and evil slightly. Know the tides through which we move.

The last sentence is quietly ominous. The tides through which we move--the highs and the lows, the peaks and the troughs-- tell us repeatedly that nothing lasts and that all life ends in death. Let us temper our excitement and agitation, whether for the ecstasy of battle or the ecstasy of sex, whether over great achievement or great loss, and admit to ourselves that all things have their moment and are gone. If we live according to this sober knowledge, we will live as well as we can.[13]

Reflecting on Philosophy In the Dungeon

This energetic appreciation of human life may well present the possibility of a radical departure from your current status quo. The materialistic outlook of our Western society would easily dismiss ideas such as chakras and energy exchange as so much "New Age woo-woo," as corny and fabricated as a midway con artist.

For a moment, though, remove your rose-colored glasses and try to sense your own vibratory rate. How fast or slow, deep or shallow is your breath? Can you quiet yourself enough to hear the beat of your own heart? Find your pulse and feel it in your wrist, in your groin, or in your neck.

What spoke to you in this chapter? Which sentences seemed real to you? When did you think "Yes I believe that"? How then can you increase your awareness of yourself as an energetic entity? How can you improve the flow of energy in your life, especially in your sexual activity? When you share your body with your partner what more can you share? How can you make it more than physical or sexual? Do you, can you, recognize sexual activity as intellectual, emotional, or spiritual?

1   For more information about this famous formula, I recommend Dennis Overbye's *Einstein in Love : A Scientific Romance*, published by Penguin in 2001.

2   Joy, MD, W. Brugh, J*oy's Way, A Map for the Transformational Journey,* Jeremy P. Tarcher, Inc., Los Angeles, 1979.

3   *The Principles of Tantra*, frontispiece.

4   Rinella, Jack, *Partners in Power*, Greenery Press, Oakland, CA, 2003, pages 170-171.

5   Krishna, Gopi, *A Kundalini Catechism*, The Kundalini Research Foundation, Ltd., Darien, CT, 1995, page 2.

6   Thompson, Mark, *Gay Soul, Finding the Heart of Gay Spirit and Nature,* HarperCollins, San Francisco, 1995, pages 205-206.

7   *The Principles of Tantra,* page 320.

8   *The Principles of Tantra,* frontispiece.

9   Hill, Napoleon, etc.

10   I suggest the book that started me out on my understanding of visualization: Shakti Gawain's *Creative Visualization: Use the Power of Your Imagination to Create What You Want in Your Life,* 25th anniversary edition, published by New World Library, 2002.

11   Romans 8:28, *Revised Standard Version.*

12   Krishnamurti, *At the Feet of the Master,* Yogi Publication Society, Chicago, pages 55-56.

13   *Sailing the Wine-Dark Sea,* page 100.

Chapter

A Pause to Reflect   5

Arriving at a valid philosophy of what it is that we do demands that we first acknowledge what may be deeply seated beliefs that condemn BDSM activity and contradict the premises upon which such activity might be justified. Having begun to do that, we can replace them with paradigms that are more consistent with our innate understanding of who we are and what we do. At the same time we need to ground our philosophy in life experience, scientific fact, and correct logic.

By insisting as I have that our investigation of sex and spirituality ought to be holistic I am challenging what seems to be a popular assumption made by most contemporary religions; that is, I am denying the preeminence of scripture, be it Bible, Koran, Veda, or any other sacred writing, as well as that of religious authority, be he or she pope, pastor, ayatollah, guru, or any other prophet. I write this because the primary basis of our analysis needs to be holistic itself; each aspect has a place in our discussion, and to allow any one discipline to take precedence skews the discussion in a prejudicial, and therefore blinding, manner.

Here then we can see the influence of the subculture of BDSM as I know it. I have often written that what sets us apart is that we are a community of rugged individualists, men and women who listen to a different drummer, willing to search out our unique and personal path whether it be sexual, communal, or spiritual.

I am not denying the value of either scripture or authority. Instead I am elevating the role of the individual to discern spiritual and sexual truth for his or her own self. This is not to make personal revelation primary either, but rather to acknowledge the necessity of considering sex and spirit in a multi-dimensional, inter-disciplinary way. More importantly it is meant to emphasize the freedom that the individual has to seek and worship divinity on his or her own terms, to live a spiritual life according to spirit as he or she knows it, not as imposed by doctrine, culture, or other external pressures.

Rather than accepting one paradigm (history as linear, for instance) or another (history is cyclical), perhaps there is something to be said about reflecting on both, incorporating them together if possible, or even creatively arriving at a third paradigm through reason, experience, or synthesis.

I'm sure you've heard the story of the five blind men who inspected an elephant. Each reported his experience to the king as a description of the elephant as he had experienced it. For one, then, it was like the elephant's ear, for another like the leg, a tail, its side, or a tusk. Each in his own way was correct but only to a point, since obviously an elephant has each of those characteristics and is still more than the sum of those parts. Too often we fail to remember that our ability to "see" the whole is woefully inadequate. We accept separateness as reality when connectedness is fundamental to all existence. We put our religious lives in one distinct category, our sexual ones in another, our scientific ones in a third, and so forth, when we ought rather to grasp their inter-relatedness, that each way of knowing has its own contribution to add to our knowing.

Likewise I believe that science can and should add its perspective to this investigation. The conflicts between Science and Religion are only in appearances caused by knowledge that is incomplete. The quest for truth ought not be limited by the prejudice of a "scientific method" or a "faith-based" appreciation of reality. It is no surprise to me, for instance, that Einstein's Theory of Relativity supports the Eastern concept of the human body as being composed of energy centers.

History, too, casts its own understanding into the investigation, especially as it sheds light on the strong connection between religion and political power. Whereas one would expect (or at least hope) that spirituality would lead to freedom, instead we find its shadow, i.e., religion, leading to control of the individual by a priestly, shamanic, or ministerial class. One might look for faith to empower the believer but too often the effect of faith is the subjugation of the believer to the will of another, the most extreme examples being the Inquisition, martyrdom, and forced baptism. Imagine for a moment, for example, how different our Western society would be if the Canaanites had withstood the Hebrews or if our church services were as sexual as practiced in the temples of Sumer.

It is exactly this openness to a richness, fullness, and variety of faith that I believe each seeker must have in order to arrive at holiness. This is not a holiness gained by another's decree or dogma, nor a holiness that mirrors this prophet or that saint, but rather a holiness that arises out of the wholeness of the individual. In this regard authenticity to one's self is what is necessary.

Herein we find the most personal of relationships between God and man, that every person knows the divine life that constitutes the very being of their being and is one with that being, knowing self and being true to the self that one knows.

Reflecting on Philosophy In the Dungeon

How do you approach sex and spirituality? Is it out of curiosity or for serious study? What do you think? Answer yourself truthfully, as that is hardly a rhetorical question.

Chapter

Unity 6

To understand the conjunction of sex and spirit it matters less whether you believe in one God or many than that you have an understanding of the fundamental Unity of all existence, which is to say that Reality is connected in myriad ways so that no aspect of it is independent of any other.

The Experience of BDSM

Not only is the acknowledgement of a unified existence fundamental to our philosophical understanding, it is also experientially a significant part of what we learn in the dungeon. We don't necessarily state it in the terms given above, but a significant sensation often found in SM-related experiences is a profound sense of unity, of being one with the Universe.

As with most of us, I have experienced this unity while in bondage, toward the high point of an effective flogging scene, and during ejaculation and the after-glow of orgasm. Though I experienced much of this as a bottom, my years as a top have afforded me similar sensations.

For me, the act of submitting to the ropes and restraints of a bondage scene is a liberating experience. The times I have been mummified in plastic wrap and duct tape I have found myself drifting ever more deeply into an immense space of quiet peace. Unable to move my body in the physical world, my mind descends into an alpha state and then into theta reverie. Unencumbered by the ability or need to do anything or even to maintain consciousness of my surroundings, I enter into a deeply meditative state. Blindfolded, my eyes first see only darkness and then experience the peaceful expanse of a star-lit panorama.

In time one of those "stars" expands in brightness and often takes on the image of an eye, occasionally even reminiscent of the Egyptian "Eye of Horus." In deeper states I can hear soft music. My feeling of self as a distinct entity dissipates into a strong sense of bonding with all that is. I am no longer alone but am rather one with all that I "see."

A good flogging has a similar effect. The impact of the leather thongs slowly causes my nervous system to release endorphins into my blood stream, leading once again to a deeply secure and safe feeling as I float in a sea of tranquility. These dungeon experiences offer insight into and affirm the basic unity upon which a philosophy of kink rests.

Oneness

 To put it another way there is one basis for all being. That basis is God by whatever word we use to describe the Ultimate, Supreme, and Un-caused Cause, that Being which is the ground, the being-ness, of all Being and therefore of all beings. Being-ness encompasses all states and forms of being. Everything, then, is an expression, a manifestation, of *That Which Is* and without the presence of *That Which Is* nothing is. To take this one step further, even nothing, as a state, exists because of the presence of That Which Is. Hence in the ultimate analysis, God is in all and all are in God.

The world of conventional, everyday experience appears as a multitude of separate things extended in space and succeeding one another in time. Their existence is always realized by contrast or opposition. That is to say, we realize or isolate the experience of light by contrast with darkness, pleasure with pain, life with death, good with evil, subject with object. Opposition, duality, is therefore the inevitable condition of this world, however much we may struggle to overcome it, to hold to the pleasant and the good and to reject the painful and the evil -- an effort which is of necessity a vicious circle, since without pain pleasure is meaningless. However, this world of opposites is conventional and "seeming"; it is not the real world. For reality is neither multiple, temporal, spatial, nor dual. Figuratively speaking, it is the One rather than the Many. But it appears to be the Many by a process variously described as manifestation, creation by the Word, sacrificial dismemberment, art, play, or illusion -- to name but a few of the terms by which the doctrine accounts for the existence of the conventional world.

> In sum then, the manifold world of things proceeds from the One and returns to the One, though in actuality it is never at any time other than the One save in play, "art", or seeming. Its coming from and returning to the One, its Alpha and Omega, appears to be a temporal process because the "art" by which it is manifested involves the convention of time. So long as the human mind is enchanted by this "art", it takes the convention for the reality and, in consequence, becomes involved in the tormenting vicious circle of wrestling with the opposites, of the pursuit of pleasure and the flight from pain. But one may be liberated or saved from this everlasting (circular) torment by disenchantment, by seeing through the illusion.[1]

This understanding of the unity of Being-ness has profound implications for us as humans. Understanding this, we can understand ourselves as a manifestation of divinity. It is literally true that God is in us, that we are of God. In his commentary on *The Bhagavad Gita*, Eknath Easwaran echoes these sentiments:

I have described the discovery of Atman and Brahman -- God immanent and God transcendent -- as separate, but there is no real distinction. In the climax of meditation, the sages discovered *unity:* the same indivisible reality without and within. It was *advaita,* "not two." The Chandogya Upanishad says epigrammatically, *Tat tvam asi:* "Thou art That." Atman is Brahman: the Self in each person is not different from the Godhead.

Nor is it different from person to person. The Self is one, the same in every creature. This is not some peculiar tenet of the Hindu scriptures; it is the testimony of everyone who has undergone these experiments in the depths of consciousness and followed them through to the end. Here is Ruysbroeck, a great mystic of medieval Europe; every word is carefully chosen:

The image of God is found essentially and personally in all mankind. Each possesses it entire and undivided, and all together not more than one alone. In this way we are all one, intimately united in our eternal image, which is the image of God and the source in us of all our life.[2]

For some, of course, the concept of a person being divine is blasphemous. Those holding such a view see God as distinctly Other, Supreme, while humans are less than divine, weighed down by ungodly flesh, mired in sin which is, they believe, antithetical to God's existence. This paradigm is based on anthropomorphic concepts of Divinity, that is, we attribute human qualities to God, such as fatherhood, and endow God with characteristics such as gender, personality, and a beard. The Old Testament portrayal of the God of Moses as YHWH -- I am -- has given place to the jealous caricature called Jehovah.

God's infinity, so to speak, has been emasculated as Godhood is seen as encompassing a goodness, blessedness, and holiness that is no longer whole. The Hindus have not lost sight of the infinity of God:

> All that is manifest is Power (Sakti) as
> Mind, Life and Matter. Power implies a Power-Holder
> (Saktiman). There is no Power-Holder without Power,
> or Power without Power-Holder. The Power-Holder
> is Siva. Power is Sakti, the Great Mother of the
> Universe. There is no Siva without Sakti, or Sakti
> without Siva. The two as they are in themselves are
> one. They are each Being, Conscious-ness and Bliss.
> These three terms are chosen to denote ultimate
> Reality, because Being or "Is-ness" as distinguished
> from particular forms of Being, cannot be thought
> away. "To be" again is "to be conscious" and lastly
> perfect Being-Consciousness is the Whole and
> unlimited unconstrained Being is Bliss. These three
> terms stand for the ultimate creative Reality as it
> is in itself. By the imposition upon these terms of
> Name (Nama) and Form (Riipa) or Mind and Matter,
> we have the limited Being-Consciousness and Bliss
> which is the Universe.[3]

God, then, is not separate from creation but is the fundamental essence of creation. This is not a creation limited by what we know of it, but rather the totality of all that is and is not, far beyond the imagination of our limited faculties of intellect. It is not as we perceive it, since our ability to perceive is limited.

> The relevance of *za-zen* [meditation
> or "sitting Zen"] to Zen is obvious when it is
> remembered that Zen is seeing reality directly, in
> its "suchness." To see the world as it is concretely,
> undivided by categories and abstractions, one must
> certainly look at it with a mind which is not thinking
> -- which is to say, forming symbols -- about it. *Za-zen*
> is not, therefore, sitting with a blank mind which

excludes all the impressions of the inner and outer
senses. It is not "concentration" in the usual sense
of restricting the attention to a single sense *object,*
such as a point of light or the tip of one's nose.
It is simply a quiet awareness, without comment,
of whatever happens to be here and now. This
awareness is attended by the most vivid sensation
of "nondifference" between oneself and the external
world, between the mind and its contents -- the
various sounds, sights, and other impressions of the
surrounding environment. Naturally, this sensation
does not arise by trying to acquire it; it just comes by
itself when one is sitting and watching without any
purpose in mind -- even the purpose of getting rid of
purpose.[4]

The idea of fundamental unity is difficult for those of a
Western worldview to remember as we consider spiritual matters.
Even our fundamental thought patterns reflect the duality of good
and evil and right and wrong. In a white Anglo-Saxon culture, to
hear, for instance, the word "black" is to think evil, while white
forever connotes "pure." Obviously other cultures have different
perceptions. In some cultures, for instance, white, not black, is
the color of mourning. What is necessary is to constantly remind
ourselves that All is One and that God, by whatever name we use,
is in All as All is in God.

The importance of "grasping" this understanding is that
by doing so we understand the connectedness of all existence.
Nothing is separated from anything else, there are only degrees of
distance between related entities and activities. A stone dropped
in Cleveland sends a wave through the planet. Theoretically it
would be felt in China, if only our listening devices were sensitive
enough.

In this sense Oneness means that opposites are merely
opposite sides of the same greater entity. They are in fact co-
existent within the One, hence both good and evil, black and white,

higher and lower, action and inaction, for examples, are united in Reality, therefore resolving, as incomprehensible as it may seem to a mind steeped in duality, all conflict.

Hence Apollo and Dionysos, order and chaos, comedy and tragedy all exist within Reality, even if we perceive such existence as distinct and separate. It is within this context that the Greek god Dionysos, son of Zeus and Semele, union of Father God and Human Mother, manifests in his oneness unity. As can be seen in the ancient Greek play, *Bakkhoi, The Followers of Bacchus* (the Roman name for Dionysos), he is both comic and tragic, bringing both joy and destruction, much in the same way as the Hindu Deity Shiva is both destroyer and creator. Such dualities are seen repeatedly in agrarian societies, as the earth must be plowed in order to be sown, the seed must be planted (die) in order to sprout (live). These themes are repeated in the Old Testament book of Ecclesiastes as well, "For everything there is a season, and time for every matter under heaven."[5]

Western thought is forever mindful of the laws of economics -- the allocation of limited resources among competing needs -- but from the Universe's viewpoint we are never dealing with limit or competition. We too often see the answer as either/or, refusing to envision the infinity of the whole, that possibilities are in fact endless. Our materialistic point of view limits us to the experience of this plane, that which is scientifically and empirically demonstrable, without remembering that there are multitudes of planes in which other realities, even realities which may affect us, exist.

We act as if our perceptions are always true, always correct, always whole, when in fact they are always only partly true, therefore always not quite correct, and never complete. Our perceptions are certainly helpful but not really helpful enough. We must constantly remind ourselves that what we perceive is only what we perceive and never the totality of what it is that we are perceiving.

91

We must then take off our blinders, our rose-colored glasses, and attempt to grasp the fullness of possibilities. It is not, nor has it ever been, necessary to worship only Apollo or Dionysos. There is no one way but rather there are many ways. It is not faith in a specific dogma, ritual, or worldview that matters but rather faith in one's dogma, ritual, or worldview. As long as we perceive our alienation as separateness, we embrace a monotheism that denies the fullness of being, the fullness of Reality, indeed the true infinity and power of the Divine.

That's not to say that we don't suffer from alienation but that we suffer from it because we fail to see the fundamental and essential unity that we share with that from which we think we are alienated, even while we realize our separateness and embrace the individuality that is therefore created. We ought to celebrate that which we are, knowing that we are also defined by that which we are not.

Polarity and Duality

I am not making the argument that duality does not exist, as indeed our experience of duality is rather forceful. Instead I am saying that duality proceeds from unity, that our focus on duality is a fundamental illusion which is part and parcel of our human existence. True knowing, then, requires that we be disillusioned, i.e., that we break through the illusion and see reality as it is. That which is One contains within itself the two and so our consideration of Unity leads us to duality.

> At the very roots of Chinese thinking and feeling there lies the principle of polarity, which is not to be confused with the ideas of opposition or conflict. In the metaphors of other cultures, light is at war with darkness, life with death, good with evil, and the positive with the negative, and thus an idealism to cultivate the former and be rid of the latter flourishes

throughout much of the world. To the traditional way of Chinese thinking, this is as incomprehensible as an electric current without both positive and negative poles, for polarity is the principle that + and -, north and south, are different aspects of one and the same system, and that the disappearance of either one of them would be the disappearance of the system.[6]

In Chinese the two poles of cosmic energy are *yang* (positive) and *yin* (negative) , and their conventional signs are respectively - and --.The ideograms indicate the sunny and shady sides of a hill, *fou,* and they are associated with the masculine and the feminine, the firm and the yielding, the strong and the weak, the light and the dark, the rising and the falling, heaven and earth, and they are even recognized in such everyday matters as cooking as the spicy and the bland. Thus the art of life is not seen as holding to *yang* and banishing *yin,* but as keeping the two in balance, because there cannot be one without the other. When regarding them as the masculine and the feminine, the reference is not so much to male and female individuals as to characteristics which are dominant in, but not confined to, each of the two sexes. Obviously, the male has the convex penis and the female the concave vagina; and though people have regarded the former as a possession and the latter as a deprivation (Freud's "penis envy"), any fool should be able to recognize that one cannot have the outstanding without the instanding, and that a rampant *membrum virile* is no good without somewhere to put it, and vice versa. But the male individual must not neglect his female component, nor the female her male. Thus Lao-tzu says:

> Knowing the male but keeping
> the female, one becomes a universal stream.
> Becoming a universal stream, one is not
> separated from eternal virtue.[7]

Since the dominant cultures of the world are based on a heterosexual model of sexuality, it is to be expected that gender would play an important part in their understanding of polarity. That does not, though, eliminate the possibility of there being polarity in same sex relationships as well, since a person of either gender has the capacity to realize and manifest various aspects of either gender. There is, after all, a distinction between male and masculine as there is between female and feminine. I am sure that I don't have to remind you that a person of either gender (and I could just as comfortably write a person of any gender) has characteristics that we culturally apply to one gender or the other.

What is necessary is to understand that there are multiple potentials, many combinations that we can explore, not just male/female, but male/male, female/female, and variations of those themes, including the masculine, the feminine, the dominant and submissive, the aggressive and the passive, and the Transgendered, Bisexual, and multi-faceted nuances that can be found in all relationships.

The man or woman with true spiritual sight sees, then, that there are equal opposites and that the goal is to achieve this recognition and thus bring the balance that restores unity. There is no longer a struggle between God and Satan, between spirit and flesh. In his book *Gay Soul*, interviewer and author Mark Thompson asks James Broughton:

> Is there any separation between the soul and the body?

Broughton replies:

> "Those who see any difference between the soul and the body have neither," said Oscar Wilde. The soul expresses itself throughout the body, in its members, organs, nerves, and cells, in all actions

of desire, daring, and droop, wherever you ache
and wherever you soar. Every nook and cranny of
yourself can flutter and stretch, exude and hum, in
experiencing the pleasures and pains of being alive.
The body is a holy place of romp and renewal. It is
not the shameful sewer that orthodox religions insist
upon. Novalis said, "There is only one temple in the
world, and that is the human body." From your tiptoe
to your topknot you are throbbingly alive in the dance
of the divine mystery.

   The genitals, the anus, and the perineum are
the holy trinity at the root of your torso's experience.
The penis is the exposed tip of the heart and the wand
of the soul. The perineum animates all the chakras.
The anus is the transforming and recycling volcano
that fertilizes new growth.

   The proper activity in a temple is worship.
Open your temple to love. Visit other temples. In my
temple the names of gaiety's trinity are Always, Mary,
and Bright.[8]

   This appreciation of the unity of All eliminates the
body/spirit conflict that is rampant in the world. Sex and the body
are no longer dirty; spirit is no longer better and higher, cut off
from the physical. Instead they are mutually bound in the glorious
celebration of human (and indeed all) life.

   This appreciation allows us to resolve what appears as
conflict. We are mindful that categories are no more than helpful
handles to speak; they are somehow basic to our thinking patterns,
but categories are just that: categories. Creation is not merely a
collection of categories. Instead categories are ways that we can
comprehend (though in a limited way) creation.

   What, for instance, does this say of the differences, easily
perceived as conflict, between Dionysos, the mad god, and his
half brother Apollo, the god of order? Once again we return to the
necessity of understanding the unity, just as the worship at Delphi,

the ancient temple of renowned seers, was dedicated to both Apollo and Dionysos. The seers sought knowledge from Dionysos in the winter months, from Apollo the rest of the year. Both Apollonian order and Dionysian chaos are necessary if there is to be balance. It seems to me, then, that we must recognize and practice both, even as the New Testament quotes Jesus, "Render unto Caesar the things that are Caesar's and to God the things that are God's."[9]

Alienation

Though I can take exception to much that Karl Marx believed, it is obvious that we all suffer a great deal from a sense of alienation, the gnawing knowledge that we are separate from one another, as well as from our environment and even (especially) the core of our own being. As we read in Genesis "It is not good for man to be alone," we deeply feel that aloneness. Our desire for unity, expressed in a need to belong, to be part of a common unity, to be accepted and loved, is therefore a great driving force in all we do.

To reiterate what I wrote before, understanding our unity with all Being is the basis for dissolving and soothing our feeling of being separate.

The gift of sexual activity is one way, albeit often not very successful, for us to experience the momentary bliss of connection. Likewise religious observance is meant to connect us to the divine, ending our separation from the very ground, the substance of who we are. It is no wonder that the purpose of faith is to reconcile us with God. Here then we see the fundamental commonality of sex and spirit -- to bring us to completion, that is into relationship with other and Other. Is there any wonder then that ancient religious practices were sexual?

Reflecting on Philosophy In the Dungeon

I find it a shame that monotheism as believed by the great religions of our day is so little reflected in an understanding of our fundamental unity, that we are One. Fearful of pantheism and the deification of Man, those who believe in the one God would have us believe that we are split apart from the Oneness we share with that God and with one another.

Likewise Western religion's renunciation of fertility rites, their glorification of Jehovah and therefore God the Father to the denial of the Goddess, has driven a great divide between sex and spirit. Sexual activity, which could be such a strong force for realizing our unity, for strengthening and revealing the bonds we share, is instead made dirty, shameful, sinful, and evil, becoming a force for darkness and separation rather than for love and unity.

How does the feeling of separation affect you? How does what you believe alleviate or contribute to that alienation? How do your sexual experiences provide a sense of bonding, of togetherness, and of unity for you? If they don't, what do you believe that keeps them from bringing that experience of unity to you?

1   Watts, Alan, *Myth and Ritual in Christianity*, Beacon Press, Boston, 1968, page 17.

2   *The Bhagavad Gita*, pages xxiii-xxiv.

3   Avalon, Arthur, *The Serpent Power, The Secrets of Tantric and Shakti Yoga,* Dove Publications, New York, 1974, page 23.

4   *The Way of Zen*, pages 155-156.

5   Ecclesiastes 3:1, *Revised Standard Version.*

6   Watts, Alan, with the collaboration of Al Chung-liang Huang, Tao, *The Watercourse Way*, Pantheon Books, New York, 1975, pages 19-20.

7   *The Watercourse Way*, Pages 21-22.

8   *Gay Soul,* HarperCollins, 1995, pages 11-12.

9   Matthew 22:21, *King James Version.*

Life As Process

If your childhood was anything like mine, you were told stories about princes and princesses. Those fairytales and others like them contained a message that I think is very misleading: No matter what the circumstances, we can get to live happily ever after. Life by that standard is a project. Once a certain task is done we can rest safely in our castles for evermore.

I guess that's fine if we want to bring closure to the reading of a book or the telling of a story, but the simple fact of the matter is that life isn't a closed-end, someday-done process where we will have arrived at some grand moment of final contentment. I'm not about to push this idea past the breathing of one's last breath, since I haven't yet experienced and am no authority on life after death, but life is a process, not a project.

In the twentieth century, Constantine Cavafy, a native of Alexandria who wrote in modern Greek, saw the *Odyssey* as a metaphor for the journey of life, the end of the journey being not nearly as important as the journey itself. In his much-quoted poem "Ithaca," he advises the reader:

Hope the way is long.
May there be many summer mornings
        when,
with what pleasure, with what joy,
you shall enter first-seen harbors...
Keep Ithaca always in your mind.
Arriving there is what has been ordained

for you.
But do not hurry the journey at all.
Better if it lasts many years;
and you dock an old man on the island,
rich with all that you've gained on the way,
not expecting Ithaca to give you wealth.
Ithaca gave you the beautiful journey.
Without her you would not have set out.
She has nothing more to give you.[1]

The idea of life as process has significance as to how we live life and what it is that we do in that living. You see, there is no ending point (short of death) where we can say we have finally arrived at The Goal. It's not the "there" of getting there that counts but the "getting." It is the doing, not the having done, that matters.

Let's look at it another way: In reality, though one would sometimes never suspect it, sexual intercourse isn't just about having an orgasm. In fact there are some who have sex and seldom have an orgasm, yet they enjoy the sex they have. There are others, like myself, who have very satisfying orgasms but who take great delight in all the play that leads up to the final moment of shooting one's load or wetting one's pussy. As a matter of fact I have learned (though I don't always practice what I've learned) to delay ejaculation so I can enjoy multiple orgasms. I'd rather play at the edge for hours than experience that momentary and its-soon-over-pleasure of "le petit mort."

For me, even orgasm is not the end of sex as I choose to bask in its glow and explore the sensations and states into which it has thrust me. Thus you can see that for me the process is more important than the accomplishment. That said, I am a project-oriented person and do enjoy the satisfaction of a job well done.

Of course we don't act as if life is process. We hold the Old Guard[2] in awe as if they knew something that we don't and deceive ourselves that if we could only figure out the right protocols or find the right partner or learn the right technique, all would be well. The fallacy is in thinking "If only I could arrive." Bull shit. There will always be another layer of life into which we can delve more deeply. We never get there, at least as long as we breathe on this planet in this universe. It is the voyage, not the destination that counts.

This viewpoint has many ramifications for our kinky subculture, though I could have just as easily and correctly written "ramifications for all living creatures." It means that change is our only constant. Our groups, our friendships, our significant relationships, our play and their attendant scenes, our desires, goals, and levels of experience will all evolve. Education is a process that never ends. Experience is a process that in itself changes us and sets the stage for newer experiences.

It is, then, a matter of change and (we hope) growth, of refining and perfecting, even if we reach neither pure refinement nor perfection. We can, of course, stay stuck in the mud, refuse to learn important lessons, and generally stagnate in our self-created mire. Likewise we can take a deep breath, remind ourselves that it is only change and adapt into the new us we were always meant to become. Dealing with change is no easy matter. After all, the status quo often appears to be the most comfortable of places.

As I watch the vegetables in my garden grow, I can imagine the struggle they endure to break open their seed coverings and push through the soil. I see them reach for sun and know that some nights it really is too cold out there for them, though they survive. I want them to be full grown and harvestable right now, but that's not the case.

I have to water them, add fertilizer, pull weeds, prune unwanted shoots and thin seedlings that are too crowded. Only daily attention to my 20 by 20 foot plot will ensure a good harvest. Only attention to your process will guarantee the momentary satisfaction of a leather-life well-lived. Yes, satisfaction is momentary, but thankfully, so are the bad times as well, even if those moments seem to last excruciatingly long. Hang on to the roller coaster, friends, as a life in leather can be a thrilling ride.

The cerebral side of what we do forms a strong foundation for the rest of our lifestyle. What then does looking at life as a process rather than a project mean when it comes to being kinky? The short answer is that it means a great deal, since such an outlook colors everything we experience. Allow me to illustrate it in terms of finding, meeting, and playing, though it applies to much more, such as negotiating or organizing and running a club.

Finding

One of the more consistent questions that fills my email inbox is "Jack, how do I find a partner?" The short answer is "Type 'BDSM,' the name of your city or area and the word 'munch' into a search engine." The resulting list is a place for your search to start. Even if you aren't computer savvy your local librarian can help you out in that regard.

For those less experienced in the vocabulary of kink, a munch is a gathering of kinky folk held in a public venue such as a restaurant so that interested parties can meet the group and one another in a safe, non-threatening environment.

Review what you've found. There may be a newsgroup you can join and lurk in, or an invitation to a public gathering of some sort, or the contact name for a local group. The process will now continue as you explore each venue to find the one where you are most comfortable. It is, though, a process. Don't expect that the first group you find will be the right one for you. Rather it will simply be a place to start and to gather initial information.

If you don't like what you find, move on and look again or bear with it and see what happens. Use your encounter not as the end of your search but as a means to learning more. It is all part of the process. Learning what you don't like, after all, is just as important as discovering what you do.

The general process resembles my search for salamanders

at the age of twelve or thirteen. It was then that my mom let me cross the street and explore the fields and ravines that earlier had been off-limits. Once there I found a lot of small streams, filled with rocks and sand. Turning over a rock might reveal a salamander. The more rocks I unearthed, the more salamanders I could capture to bring home. It was a numbers game.

Likewise, finding is a numbers game, even when you think that there is nothing to be found. I am reminded of a guy from Tulsa whom I met online. He complained that there were no kinky men where he lived. It so happened that I was going to Oklahoma City to speak and I invited him to join me for the weekend. He did and met several people who could act as his entrée into our scene.

The punch line to the story is that some of the people he "met" were already his friends, as they were from his home town and patronized many of the places with which he was already familiar. It was strange to think that it took a guy from Chicago (me) to introduce him to people he already knew in Oklahoma.

What if he had met no one from his hometown? He would then have to search for other alternatives, knowing that he had learned he might not find anyone this way, except for me, of course. He would have to evaluate his process for insight as to what he had to change in his seeking, perhaps by widening his search criteria or looking for another source of information. Seeing that finding is a process means that failure leads to success, if one but perseveres in the process. Even finding isn't the end of the process. It simply leads to a different process.

Meeting

We often approach meeting someone as a one-time event. We are introduced, shake hands and greet, exchange some pleasantries and think that we have met them. Project over -- NOT. It is more the reality that the process is one of "Getting to know

103

you, getting to know all about you." Even when we meet someone who is not the person we are seeking, it is important to remember that this meeting can, when we see it as process, lead us closer to the one we are seeking.

The process approach, then, is to open yourself to learning, to growing, to exploring without prejudice, always looking for the next lead, the next meeting. It also means that we see each person as an ally, a potential partner, a possible mentor, guide, or teacher. Each new acquaintance can be a link in a network that, as we move across its nodes, leads us to more possibilities, more people, and therefore closer to our goal.

Unfortunately we too often think and therefore act as if meeting the "wrong" person is a failure, while if we see it as part of our process that person may be just the very person to introduce us to the one whom we seek. Every slave applicant, for instance, ought to ask masters who are uninterested in them if they can lead them to another master who might be the right one.

I met Matthew because he had met my friend Master Vince. Even though they didn't hit it off in terms of a relationship, Vince was kind enough to point Matt in my direction. Rather than being a failed meeting for them it turned out to be just the meeting that Matt needed in order to meet me.

Playing

What we do is a process. From negotiating to setting the scene, to warming up to the heart of the fetish, and to aftercare, playing is a process. It's not just a one-time process either, as successive scenes are always going to build upon the ones that went before even as they are stepping stones to the ones that will come later.

That's why I always see the first and second times I play with someone as just the beginning. First scenes are generally light and highly exploratory. Second scenes are more comfortable since each of us has some knowledge of what might happen. Third scenes are the ones that really get down to business. In fact it is usually only then that two people can begin to play in earnest, trust and security having been built during encounters one and two.

To think that the first time, or even the second, is what you're after negates the opportunity for more and often improved encounters later. If you think your projects are always failing, then see them as processes that are winning because they contain information that may lead to success at the next try.

Be consistent in spending time analyzing your experiences, seeking to grasp the lessons that each moment holds. Discuss scenes with your partners, share your fantasies, ask your questions, probe for meaning either by discussion, research, contemplation, or in a journal. That way, you'll have a better chance at gaining the prize -- no matter what it is you're seeking.

Education

The privilege of public speaking, at least to the friendly folks who listen so attentively, ask lots of great questions, and generally treat me like a celebrity, is really an opportunity for me to learn. Most students probably don't realize that teachers are the ones who learn the most in the classroom when they teach.

If I didn't have to write weekly, which I see as a form of teaching, I wouldn't put so much thought into the kinky activity of which I write, I wouldn't be getting the great questions that prompt me to think more deeply about what it is that we do, and I certainly wouldn't have the privilege of so many chances to observe the scene -- one of my favorite occupations -- a viewing that allows me the rare opportunity to compare my experiences with others' and to analyze our differences and observe our similarities. The likes and un-likes are especially notable when I join my pansexual friends at their conventions.

There's a man coming around who has been thinking and reading about our scene for several years but who has (as he acknowledges) little experience. He's asked me to teach him, something I am very happy to do for a lot of reasons.

So I reminisce about how I learned my Leather basics in the early and mid-eighties and it looks almost nothing like the pedagogy I find in our presentations and seminars today. Yes, presentations were popularized by Gay events such as the Chicago Hellfire Club's Inferno, and, yes, The Gay Male SM Activists of New York (GMSMA) organized as an educational group, but historically most of my generation of Gay Leathermen learned how to be what we wanted to be -- Leathermen -- by a loose kind of mentoring.

I use the word "loose" because I don't want to imply any kind of systemization or organization. I don't think my mentors would have ever thought of themselves as such and I certainly didn't think of them in that way either. The only title I ever bestowed on the two men whom today I consider my most important mentors was that of "fuck-buddy." Most of the others I can only say were "tricks" (as I was to them) and I find nothing at all derogatory in that title. I was privileged that they took me home with them for an educational and very enjoyable night.

In both cases, the goal was not to learn but to get it on and get off. It's obvious, though, that with a newbie like I was then, some things had to be explained before they could be done. Those scenes became intimate demos where I was both the subject and the student. It was like having my cake and eating it too.

So I became a Leatherman through many hands-on experiences: rope in Philadelphia, fisting in Chicago, piss in New Orleans, needle play and sounds in Novi (a city outside of Detroit). I was lucky to have a job where I traveled for a living and even luckier to have met many honorable, fun-loving, and committed Leathermen. It helped of course that they thought I was good-looking and knew that I was eager and ready for sex.

However it was Tom and Rick, those two fuck-buddies in Fort Wayne, who were most responsible for teaching me the ropes. In Rick's case the phrase is meant literally. He was a bondage enthusiast and was eager to tie me up, something he did well, and then nearly demanded that I do the same to him. There was nothing shameful about being versatile, that's for sure. In fact, for a nascent top like me, it was nearly an imperative. "Only the best bottoms," I was reminded more than once, "make it to the top."

I lived nowhere near any of the motorcycle or Leathermen's clubs of the day. If I had, there certainly would have been a pledge master ready (and demanding) to put me through my education before I could be considered for full membership. Everyone, and I mean everyone, had to start at the bottom, though many didn't stay there once they had earned their club patch.

Tom's mentoring was of a different nature. He lived in Philadelphia and came to Fort Wayne twice a year to visit his elderly mother. That duty done, he would sneak off to Henry's (a Gay-friendly bar and restaurant) where we met. Having tricked once, I became a regular host once his duties to his mother were fulfilled. He returned the favor at least one time when I visited him in Philly.

He was a committed top who knew that even tops had to share. His scene was rougher, more sadistic, and had a sterner edge to it than did Rick's. Still it was a process of my bottoming for fifteen minutes or fifteen whacks and then our literally rolling over and switching roles. It's not as if we actually counted or timed it, but I did want equal time. It was "OK I'll show you how it's done on your ass and then you can practice on mine."

Either I was more daring than most or maybe just hornier, but that's how I learned. A few books, of course, added to my education but in those days the most regular reading you could get was *Drummer Magazine* which fed the libido but not the need-to-know-technique. There were very few educational events, though a "School of Lower Education" put on by GMSMA at the now defunct Mine Shaft stands out in my memories. It was demos though, not instruction. Nevertheless it certainly gave me food for thought and gist for hard-ons.

Behind this search for education was a desire to join in,

an urge that was stronger than my fears and hesitations, one that overcame my doubts and fed my imagination. It's an education I can only encourage you to find in your time and your way. As always, be sure to have fun while you learn it. I certainly did.

Note especially that this education was predominantly, though not exclusively, experiential in nature. Without meaning to belittle the intellectual and rational modes of learning, I want to emphasize that a holistic and therefore healthy education must include physical, emotional, and spiritual experiences as well.

The Role of Trust

I am a strong believer that trust is the fundamental quality in healthy SM relationships -- in any relationship for that matter. Can you learn to trust me? What do I have to do to earn that trust?

There are other issues at play when one considers what constitutes a good educational experience. I bring my history, my needs, my lusts and desires with me when I teach. When I consider my student, it is difficult for me to separate the spiritual seeker from the beautiful man, from the object of desire, from the dominant or the submissive.

Then, too, there is no separating my self into separate selves. So when I want to teach you and mentor you, I also want to watch you, see you grow, experience you as you are, love you and play lustfully with you. There is, you should be warned, a great danger here, one that the true teacher needs to do his or her best to avoid -- the objectification of the student. I must respect you. I cannot allow my projections of what I want you to be **in any way** to hinder your being your authentic self.

It's a tough dance to dance.

I mentioned history in the above. I learned to top from other tops, and from many bottoms as well. It was not a matter of their topping me from below but of giving me the experiences I

needed so that I could own my desires and have the knowledge and the self-trust to express them.

Again, the primary quality, *sine qua non*, is trust. In this case the student must learn to trust both himself and his instructor, as well as his own instincts and intuitions. That which flows from the authentic self will not lead the student amiss. Yes, students need instruction in technique as well. Teachers, after all, come in many forms. Playing with the mentor is meant to give them that instruction.

Since I don't surrender control to the student when I mentor, I can say "No, don't hit me that way, hit me this way." Likewise I can take a crop to her and say "This is how you do it" and she can fully feel how it's done. That includes the caresses, the pain, the love, the energy, the power, the domination. The student will find that the only way (OK maybe not only but I think the BEST way to learn) is to fully embrace the experience from as many angles as possible. That is why I will act as bottom to the student -- so that she will know what it feels like to top.

The student will also have to learn what it feels like to bottom, therefore knowing both sides of the experience and hence knowing it more fully.

It is important to note here that just as we must trust, we must likewise be trustworthy. Trust-based relationships are reciprocal. Each partner has got to be able to trust the other and that can occur only when each partner demonstrates his or her trustworthiness.

Another primary quality that the teacher and student need to explore is holism. There is no separation between flesh and spirit, between desire and hesitation, between will and anxiety. That **all is one** is the first principle. That duality flows from unity is the next reality. Duality gives rise to polarity and polarity to the liberating flow of energy which returns us to unity. Here holism requires a full experience. It must be more than technique. There must be feeling, rationality, care, rhythm, and good timing to the event. Oftentimes the educational experience must be preceded by explanation and demonstration and actual practice and followed by review, correction, and further explanation.

In this process surrender is of the highest necessity. Surrender is the truly liberating process -- and one that society repeatedly teaches us NOT to do.

"There are quite a few hesitant slaves at our dungeon," writes an enquiring reader.[3] "Their main issue at not surrendering is that they feel that they will lose their individuality and respect as a person, an 'I own me!' kind of argument. They do have excellent examples of slavery in the local population but they aren't listening to what's being said on the subject. Do you happen to have an article on the subject of slavery and self-acceptance?"

"No, I don't" is the short answer, but I can certainly write one. First off, though, it's important to clarify what may be a sub-text in the above question. Not everyone is a slave or master, any more than we are all the same in any other way. In fact, few people really aspire to a D/s relationship. For whatever reason they eschew the master and slave thing, that is their prerogative.

Yes, we would like to project OUR interpretation of how this lifestyle ought to be lived onto others, but that is neither appropriate nor preferable. Let each of us find our style, and those who are compatible with it, and leave it at that. "Live and let live" is and always will be a very good way to act.

Therefore not everyone is willing to surrender to the same degree to which others aspire. It is their life, their body, and their right to give only that which they are willing to give. It is our responsibility to respect their choice, even when we think we have found a better way. Yes, the way may be better for us, but it holds no imperative to be "better" for someone else as well. This is a difficult pill to swallow. Let me illustrate it this way: in cruising a master/slave board recently I sent an email to a local gentleman, age 37, who was looking for a top. I simply asked him for what he was looking. His response was difficult: "Honestly, I'm looking for someone who's not as old as you." My first reaction, of course, is to tell the guy to wait 20 years and see if he likes to be the butt of such ageist comments. Instead I held my tongue or rather my typing fingers. I need to respect his desire for younger men. It may hurt to do so, but such is the case. End of illustration.

There are reasons, though, that surrender is a good idea, even if it's not of the D/s variety. Effective energy work requires a degree of surrender. Surrender to spirit is a prerequisite for true spiritual growth. Likewise, the best sexual encounters all have surrender as an important component, even if the degree of surrender varies from scene to scene and partner to partner.

With sex, that degree is highly dependent upon one's ability to trust his or her partner, which necessitates that your partner has demonstrated trustworthiness as well. With energy work it might be surrender to the teacher, to the divine, or simply to the universe. In any case, surrender and trust must go together. Often, in fact, a lack of surrender is caused by a lack of trust, which could be based on any number of good reasons.

For instance, we may not trust for the simple reason that we don't know enough about the person. After all, not everyone is trustworthy and degrees of trustworthiness vary as well. In many cases, too, the person we don't yet trust is ourselves. It is in that case that surrender and self-esteem or self-respect are linked. Here experience is the best teacher. As we gain confidence in experiencing the flow of energy, whether it is in BDSM, in the group, in our partner, and especially in ourselves, then surrender becomes easier. Time, here, is a big factor. One can not be expected to have trust immediately. It takes time, lots of time.

The reader mentioned above has linked surrender and respect in another way as well, when she writes "they feel that they will lose their individuality and respect as a person."

Well, if that's how they feel, that's how they feel. None of us has any control over the feelings of others. Others must deal with controlling their own emotions, though that may mean that we sometimes have to deal with the results of their emotions. Here it is more a question of allowing and, if possible, assisting the person in recognizing their own self-worth. In truth the fear that going bottom, of surrendering, of being seen in a less desirable light by others is rooted in one's self-image, which may not have a basis in reality.

I can use my own history as an example. It is no secret that I was a collared slave for some five years. What is less known is that having been such was an incredible learning experience. In fact having been a slave improves my standing in the community. I am not put down because of my submissive past. Instead I am admired for it. Even slave-applicants admire the fact that their potential master (me) was able to surrender in that way. They rightly see it as a sign of strength.

This is the paradox. Every friend I know who is collared to another in a long term relationship is a strong, self-sufficient, and responsible adult. Slavery is not for those who would escape, nor for those seeking a cure-all in their master or mistress. Look around you at the slaves who are known for their public service to our communities and you will see excellent examples of men and women who are responsible, courageous, and strong-willed. Yes they are each surrendered to their masters. They are so because they are strong enough to be so.

Surrender, the real giving of oneself to another, is not for those filled with self-doubt. It is for the strong of heart.

Strength comes only over time. Repetitive exercise builds muscle; neither wishing nor pretending does. Likewise it takes years of learning, practicing, and experiencing in the lifestyle for one to have the self-confidence needed to seek one's particular path. I write "particular path" on purpose. It is the recognition of one's unique qualities and his or her highly individualized vision. No two visions are identical. They may be complementary but they still retain their singularity.

That to which we are called to surrender is our inner self.

I know that this section of the chapter might imply that surrender is for the bottom and it is, obviously, but tops must surrender to their selves as well.

In the height of what it is that we do, we experience the best only when we surrender to the experience. When we allow the moment to transport us into another state, we are surrendering. For me it might mean growling, yelling, biting, beating, or just simply letting my dick have its way as I surrender into orgasm and ecstasy. For others it might mean relaxing into the pain, letting go of resistance, or allowing oneself to "go over the edge." In all cases it means giving up our fear and doubt, trusting ourselves, our partners, and the universe that the surrender we give will show us the light and bring us blissfully closer to enlightenment.

Some impediments to surrender are mostly situational. By that I mean that the time, place, or preparations are not yet adequate. Surrender ought not to be rushed. Just as the best sex takes time, so do productive periods of meditation or energy exchange. Some things, after all, can't be done well if one's eyes are fixed on the clock. Some places don't offer the right kind of space, be they too cold or too hot, too noisy or dirty, or lacking in attributes conducive to intimacy and an undisturbed focus. Good education, too, often requires a gradual unfolding and pre-requisites. We don't call some classes "SM 101" and others "Advanced" without good reason.

Many of us, too, have to first appreciate a topic in more abstract or observational ways, such as by reading a book about it or watching a demonstration, long before we are ready to participate in it physically. Instruction, for instance, in the locations and meaning of the chakras is probably necessary before one is able to experience them in a meaningful way, though that certainly wasn't the pedagogical route that my friend Ronn took with me.

The teacher can only point the student in what appears to be the right direction. If the student isn't ready, then he or she cannot be taught. In any case the good teacher will respect both the

113

student's speed and responses. The student is first and foremost the leader of the process. The teacher is only the guide, revealing and explaining that which the student desires to know.

When the student has questions there must be the freedom to ask them. That is the easiest way for the teacher to be able to respond with appropriate guidance. Until (and this is a long way off, if it ever occurs) the teacher and student are so advanced in their relationship that they develop a healthy intuition of what the other is thinking, the teacher usually can't read the student's mind. Yes, through experience in the process, i.e., having taught others, a good teacher knows what to expect, and there is the ability to read body language and energetic emanations but they avail for nothing if there is not true openness. That, of course, brings us back to trust, which the teacher must earn and which the student must be willing to give once the teacher has earned it.

You ought to know that a good teacher will want you to ask anything at any time, and that you can tell him anything at any time. Their responsibility as your teacher is to speak the truth to you in love, not reacting to your doubts and fears, but helping you to shed the light of truth on them, so that rather than controlling your actions, they are supports and safeguards for your desires. We are, of course, not taught to be this way and the injuries of the past certainly do not make such a course of truth easy. For that reason, the path to deep trust is slow.

Reflecting on Philosophy In the Dungeon

How has your life progressed? Do you sense it as a project or a process? What determines, for you, a successful life? Is it based on financial, familial, moral, social, power, or any other kind of motivation?

How easily do you trust? In what ways are you able to surrender? What fears hold you back from trusting more deeply or surrendering more fully? Are you trustworthy? How do you respond to your teachers? Do you approach them with fear and reservation or with trust and openness?

Of what aspects of dungeon play are you fearful? How can these fears be mitigated so that you can more fully enter into the experience of BDSM? In a similar and probably more fundamental way, what about sex itself do you fear? What old tapes about your body, your genitals, and sexual activity in general inhibit you from fully realizing the pleasure and sacredness of sex?

1   *Sailing the Wine-Dark Sea*, page 70.

2   Loosely defined, a term used to denote our predecessors in kink.

3   Much of this section on surrender can also be found in my introductory book, *Partners in Power*, Greenery Press, Oakland, 2003.

Chapter 8

Life In Stages

It is helpful to see the process which we call life as a series of stages leading to what is variously called enlightenment, nirvana, heaven, or eternal life. Though the idea that life is a process seems to contradict the notion of arriving at any one of these states, it does not eliminate the possibility of movement toward such a state. Whether any one of the "final destinations" of the soul, as posited by human thinking, is correct I cannot say. Though I believe that we humans share in an eternal life, I have no idea what form that life takes. I'm content to leave discovery of the afterlife to sometime after this life.

Progressive Dis-illusionment

In a healthy human existence, therefore, we can speak of a progression in life that leads to an ever-increasing amount of knowledge and eventually, it is hoped, to a modicum of what is called wisdom. We learn in stages, experience building upon experience, elementary knowledge forming a basis for more advanced learning. Our bodies grow and mature and gain an understanding of self and one's place in reality that forms a platform upon which we can experience further life and gain further understanding.

Author, lecturer, Leather titleholder, and professional therapist Guy Baldwin spoke of this progression in an interview with Mark Thompson:

Well, for me, the S/M experience is a kind of crucible in which I place myself, where I hope that my own impurities and illusions are somehow burned away. The experience is often --but not always -- the opportunity for me to alter my own state of consciousness and have a higher kind of awareness about the way the world is, my place in it, and the relationships between all things. So for me the S/M experience can function as a lens through which existence becomes focused, clarified, refined, and revealed.[1]

Notice that altered consciousness leads to a "higher kind of awareness… focused, clarified, refined, and revealed." Baldwin also rightly reflects an Eastern appreciation of human perception -- that it is filled with illusion.

Though illusion is a strong word, it is appropriate. My dictionary defines it, among several other ways, as "perception of something objectively existing in such a way as to cause misinterpretation of its actual nature." I am using the word "illusion" then in a Zen way, not that a certain state does not have existence, but that we perceive it differently than it actually is. Faulty perception is at the heart of illusion.

Perception is, after all, in the mind of the beholder. As I sit here typing I look out the window and see a tree in early Spring, barren of leaves and swaying in the late afternoon wind. I know the tree by the light rays that bounce off of it, reach my eyes, are translated into electromagnetic impulses of some kind, and are transmitted through my optic nerves to my brain, where they are then interpreted as a barren tree swaying in the wind. In this perception I think I see a tree. What I actually "see" are the light waves bouncing off the tree. What I know is my interpretation of the neurological impulses that reach my brain.

I am not denying the existence of the tree. I am only admitting that I don't know the tree. I know only what I perceive of it. Such an appreciation of perception likewise applies to all that I know, which is another way to say what St. Paul says, "Now we perceive darkly." This dark perception is why we cling to duality, are confused by what we perceive as contradictions, and divide Being into discordant, opposing, and contradictory entities.

If our perception of a tree is limited, how much more then is our perception of other realities, such as the star-lit sky or a drop of water? What we perceive as we perceive it is only a shadow of its reality, what might be called an illusion of the real being. When we begin to discuss spiritual topics our limited perceptions cause even more problems.

The challenge, then, is for us to become dis-illusioned, to find a way to rid ourselves of illusion and thus know Reality. Maturation, progressing through the stages of life, offers the possibility of peeling away some of the layers of illusion, of improving our perception, and hence grasping both self-knowledge and an understanding of divinity in the process.

We would do well to consider the growth that living affords us. It is a layered process, much like the removing of layers of an onion, ever approaching more closely the core, the true essence of living, though we move to a center that is infinite and therefore surrounded, so to speak, with an infinite number of layers. We can see movement from one layer to another in the concept of initiatory events.

Initiation

One of the more unfortunate losses in Western culture has been that of initiatory experiences. As we in the West have become more and more "civilized" over the millennia, our rites of passage have become more rite than right. Many of them are no longer practiced as widely as in previous centuries since families have become fragmented and cultures and traditions blended.

As an example, compare the narrations found in the Acts of the Apostles that retell the reception of the Holy Spirit by first-century believers with a description of the sacramental re-enactment of that phenomenon in any modern day Catholic church. A Pentecostal minister (in whose church many of the first-century phenomena still occur) once described the difference as like that of a frozen steak and one sizzling hot off the grill.

Aboriginal societies of all kinds are (or were) rich in giving their members initiatory experiences leading to both spiritual discovery, education in the life of the tribe, and fuller participation in the life of the community. Though some of these initiations pertain to the adolescent's entry into adulthood, there are many others that celebrate birth, growth, maturation, marriage, accession to various forms of leadership, and death.

In their book, *The Ceremonial Circle*, authors Cahill and Halpern write about two types of initiator:

> Elizabeth Cogburn tells us that there are two types of students of shamanism, the Black-Painted Face and the Red-Painted Face. The Black-Painted Face is one who has done a long apprenticeship with a respected teacher. She or he learns that there are very precise and traditional ways of being a shaman. The downfall of this approach is that it is often accompanied by a need to criticize those who have not had the same teacher or training. This method is usually controlled, direct, and piercing.
>
> The Red-Painted Face studies with many teachers along the way, but most of his or her guidance comes from the place deep inside that knows when things are right and appropriate, and from their intimate relationships with friends, family, lovers, and nature. This method is spontaneous, the energy flowing and undulating and the mode inclusive. The shamanism of cultural renewal requires many new forms to respond to the world as it is now. Since we

live in a multicultural society that is the repository of
many traditional teachings and ceremonial methods,
our circles will necessarily reflect many influences.[2]

Herein lies a dilemma. Our institutions are of the Black-
Painted Face type, usually highly structured and dogmatic in their
approach. Laws, morals, and systems are hierarchical, following
traditions and rubrics as carefully and rigorously as possible.
It is Apollo in the ascendancy, the rule of order, modeled after
Geometry and Mathematics, seeking harmony and precision.
Yet beneath this lies the shadow life of chaos, the archetypical
Dionysos, that which will not be so easily categorized, Dionysos
even revels in the diversity of American multiculturalism as group
after group vies for its view to be THE view. Groups may seem
to have Black-Painted Faces according to their own preferences,
but the mass of information and the conflicting data that flood us
in daily life are of the Red-Painted type, where even sub-societies
that seek to be closed ("protected," they would say) can hardly
achieve that exclusivity.

In our theoretical goals we are a Black-Painted culture
seeking peace and harmony as we define it. In reality, living as
we do in a highly diverse culture, we are predominantly of the
Red-Painted Face, learning from a wide range of teachers, and
experiencing our entry and our progress into BDSM in highly
eclectic doses. Though something could be certainly said for a
more studied and mentored approach, realism demands that we
live with the conditions as they are, until such time as we can
improve them, if indeed improvement is necessary.

Hindu gurus and Buddhist teachers are more commonly
in the Black-Painted Face category. In part two of Sir John
Woodroffe's *Principles of Tantra*, there is a whole chapter
dedicated to finding and serving one's guru. This tradition insists
on complete surrender and total obedience to one's teacher, who
takes on the awesome responsibility of directing and leading the

student, more properly called disciple in this context, along his spiritual path.

The purpose of spiritual initiation, in any case, is well explained by Mircea Eliade in his book, *Rites and Symbols of Initiation*. It is the process that leads the initiate into greater participation in the community and gives him or her a new status and a new understanding, especially of the spiritual underpinnings, the paradigms, of his or her culture. Initiation is meant to give the initiate an experience of the transcendent which will further his or her relationship to the divine and to the community that recognizes that divinity.

In primitive cultures these experiences are seen as visions, as flights, as death and resurrection, as encounters with ancestors, with spirits, and with archetypes of all kinds. They are personal re-enactments of the myths that are foundational to the world-view of the culture into which they are being more fully initiated and incorporated.

They all express a break with the universe of daily life. The twofold purpose of this break is obvious: it is the transcendence and the freedom that are obtained, for example, through ascent, flight, invisibility, incombustibility of the body. I need hardly add that the terms transcendence and freedom are not documented on the archaic levels of culture. But the experience is there, and that is what is important. The desire for absolute freedom -- that is, the desire to break the bonds that keep him tied to earth, and to free himself from his limitations -- is one of man's essential nostalgias. And the break from plane to plane effected by flight or ascent similarly signifies an act of transcendence; flight proves that one has transcended the human condition, has risen above it, by transmuting it through an excess of spirituality. Indeed, all the myths, the rites, and the legends that we have just reviewed can be translated as the longing to see the human body act after the manner of a spirit, to transmute man's corporal modality into the spirit's modality.

      The history of religion shows that such a desire to behave like a spirit is a universal phenomenon; it is not confined to any particular moment in the history of humanity. In the archaic religions, the shaman and the medicine man play the role of the mystics in developed religions; hence they constitute an exemplary model for the rest of the community precisely because they have realized transcendence and freedom, and have, by that fact, become like spirits and other Supernatural Beings. And there is good reason to believe that the desire to resemble Supernatural Beings has tormented man from the beginning of his history.[3]

It is one of my premises, as I hope is obvious, that our fetish play is meant to induce us into similar states. That which we call "subspace" is an experience of transcendence. Indeed those describing the experience of an intense whipping, cutting, or bondage scene often describe their experiences in just such terms. I would also posit that it is precisely because our American culture is so bereft of initiatory experiences that the ranks of our kinky subculture are so full. Not finding the transcendent in their churches, synagogues, temples, or mosques, men and women (often subconsciously) seek it in our dungeons.

Stages in BDSM

There are several ways in which this understanding of life's stages applies to us as SM practitioners. First, as kinky folk we (hopefully) will grow and change over the years as our kinky practices teach us what they have to offer. So many of us, as I did, come to Leather out of curiosity and a deep gnawing within that seeks more, though for most of us that "more" is seen simply as lust. I, for one, had no appreciation of what I was seeking when I ventured into those Leather bars in the 1980s. For all I knew, I was just horny. Initially the excitement of kinky sex was what I sought. There was not very much that was profound in this first stage.

In due time, I realized that having a relationship with my partner greatly increased the quality of our scenes. I also discovered that control was an important fetish to me and therefore began to seek a partner who would explore dominance and submission with me. It was then that our scenes entailed a greater depth.

I was amazed, for instance, by a very intense bondage and discipline scene with a submissive friend of mine. While bound he began to recount what he was experiencing, telling me what could only be called a past-life regression. Several months later, I had a similar experience when, after a scene with my friend Richard, he shared with me that during our play he saw us as re-enacting a past-life event wherein I was an Indian and he was a captive whom I was torturing. It was just such events that led me to seek bottom-side experiences, leading me to become Master Lynn's slave.

So began another "stage" which included all sorts of initiatory experiences that brought increased insight and understanding, forming much of the groundwork for this book. In the ensuing years continued experiences have expanded, clarified, and allowed me to articulate those insights. Needless to say, my own process continues.

Just as individuals go through stages so too do groups and organizations.

Scenes themselves have stages as well. Beginning with negotiations, they proceed to physical preparation, initiation of the scene, usually a warm-up period, increasing intensity, climax of some type, a cooling down period, and perhaps a follow-up time of sharing and reaching an understanding of what transpired. Understanding life as process, and that there are stages in all that we live and do, gives us a structure upon which to build our philosophy.

Awakening

Not every initiatory experience, obviously, is going to be like that of Aboriginal or Native American tribes. In fact, the reality of the wide ethnic, religious, and cultural diversity found within American society almost demands a Red-Painted Face approach. Once again we find ourselves confronting the reality of many ways and many paths.

Researching and writing this book has caused me to reflect on my own initiations and awakenings. Halfway through my senior year in college (1969), I attended a retreat where I met Ann, the most wonderful woman ever to enter my life. Though it wasn't love at first sight, in the ensuing months, our love grew and we began thinking about marriage, though we both knew it wouldn't be an immediate prospect.

The second half of one's senior year of college is hardly the time to be making big changes so I plugged along, finished my degree in Philosophy, got to know a lot more about Ann, job-hunted as best I could, and tried to figure out what I should do with the rest of my life.

Ann and I traveled around Vermont and New York a bit and spent some time with her family in New Jersey. It was during one of those trips that I met Cindy, a friend of hers from high school. We had spent the day in Manhattan and on the way home the two of them talked about the Catholic Pentecostal Movement, including such things as the laying on of hands, the Baptism of the Holy Spirit, miracles, the gift of tongues, and a lot about "the work that Jesus was doing in the world today." I listened carefully. Their talk was reminiscent of what I had read in the New Testament book, The Acts of the Apostles.

Later on that day, after we had dropped Cindy at her home, I asked Ann what they had been discussing. She told me and said that she, too, had been prayed over for this baptism. A week later, Ann and Cindy left for a seven week trip in Europe. While she was away I tried to find out what this movement was all about. I was very interested in Ann, but not in marrying a religious fanatic.

After graduation I began to attend prayer meetings at St. Peter's Hospital in Albany, New York and hence earned an invitation to a Full Gospel Businessman's Breakfast being held on Saturday morning in 1969 in a restaurant on Central Avenue. After the breakfast and a talk by the Reverend Harald Bredesen, I found myself sitting in the middle of a group of men with Bredesen laying his hands on me to receive this Baptism in the Holy Spirit.

I had read about Bredesen recently. It was not hard to find him mentioned in a lot of Catholic Pentecostal writing as he had been a major force in introducing the charismatic movement to my fellow Catholics. As these men gathered around me, Bredesen encouraged me to let out a joyful sound unto the Lord, so I started to hum. As I did that, I felt a tingling sensation in my feet. Quickly it moved up into my torso like raging fire and out through the top of my head. I let out a loud yell of joy. Bredesen looked at me and said, "We appreciate your enthusiasm, brother, but please keep it down a bit." I had found the fire of the Holy Spirit.

Later that afternoon I was lying on my bed when my mother came in with some laundry. We began talking and I told her what had happened. "It was like all the electricity from Niagara Falls was going through my body. If there had been a dead person in front of me," I said, "I could have touched them and they would have come alive." It was an experience that would change my life forever.

Some 35 years later, the experience is still with me and I have come to see it as both initiatory and akin to the Kundalini experience of the East. It was the most powerful of many events where I recognized the energetic realities of being a human. Though my Pentecostal friends (who haven't spoken to me in years) would adamantly deny it, this experience awakened me to myself and, I believe, eventually led me to discover and embrace many aspects of myself of which at the time I had no inkling of their existence, my sadism and my homosexuality being two of the most obvious.

I should note that as a practicing and devout Catholic I had long prayed for more of the Holy Spirit in my life. Until the beginning of the second semester of my senior year of college (right before meeting Ann) I had been studying to become a priest and repeatedly sought the Holy Spirit in my life. From the time of meeting Cindy until the experience in that restaurant I had spent considerable time reading about this Pentecostal experience, attending Pentecostal prayer meetings, and questioning those, both Catholic and Protestant, who were involved in this movement. All of this, then, can be seen as my preparation for this initiatory awakening.

What followed this Baptism was a very active participation in the religious movement, which was eventually called The Jesus Movement, with its evangelical fervor and literal interpretation of the Bible, especially the New Testament.

What I did not suspect at the time was that there also was a fundamental shift in the way I perceived the world. Without realizing it, I began to evaluate nearly every belief I held, as if I was peeling away onion-like layers of myself and the faith by which I understood life. My Catholicism gave way to Pentecostalism. The hierarchical structure of my religious life abandoned the Papacy and moved into a reliance on individual free congregations and from there into looking toward even smaller units of home-based fellowships.

Somewhere in all of this, the powerful light of that Kundalini experience went dark, as I began a struggle with my newly discovered homosexuality. Having peeled away the layers of Italian American mores and culture, I found a queer living within me. The light had exposed something in me and now I had to deal with what had been revealed, even though during the revelation itself there had been no awareness of a change in my perceptions, but change they had. In the ensuing months and years, the liberating effect of the light continued to reveal my authentic self, one that contrasted with the self I thought I was. This conflict led to what is called a "Dark Night of the Soul."

So began another initiation that lasted long, too long. Thrust into depression, nearly suicidal, divorced from Ann, estranged from our two children, terminated from my successful career, at odds with my parents and biological family, eventually I found myself apart from friends and nearing bankruptcy to boot. Even now some 23 years later I can't write about it. I retreat to my bedroom and allow soft, quiet tears to wash my face as I remember the doubt, confusion, and depression that led me to move to Chicago in 1991.

That Dark Night was a deep purge of all that I knew about myself and my life. It changed my career, altered my relationships with those I loved most, rid me of almost all of my material possessions and brought me, eventually, to rebirth as a professional writer and lecturer. I was reborn as Jack Rinella, master of Patrick and Matthew, college instructor, citizen of Chicago. Fifteen years later I am at peace with my elderly parents, and in a great relationship with my daughters and their next generation families, including grandchildren. In so many respects I am a success -- and have to admit that I live a fulfilled, fully enjoyable life, which is, of course, the true purpose of initiation.

What I have just described were two of my own awakenings, experiences that change the color of our glasses, even take them off in some mysterious way, bringing us more fully into both our own lives and the life our community. The Dark Night that precipitated and followed my divorce would be called a wound by the author and lecturer known as Ram Dass, as interviewed by Mark Thompson:

How do we use the wound for our own awakening?

Well, the question is: Who's used by it and who can use it? I would say that for many years I was used by it, and then I started to shift my consciousness and started to use it. Anybody who is awake to the human predicament of being lost in separateness starts to yearn for the truth that they are not separate, since then they are back home -- they are in harmony with things rather than always being alienated and outside. Once that awakening occurs, then it's a set of inevitable steps before you get to the point where you see your incarnation as a curriculum. You see that the ways in which you're suffering are good things to work on in yourself. In other words, you begin to understand that suffering is grace.[4]

What do you mean exactly when you use the word awaken?

There are many planes of awareness, many levels of consciousness. William James really expressed it the best. He said, "Our normal waking consciousness is but one type of consciousness, while all about it, parted from it by the filmiest of screens, there lie other types of consciousness and we spend our entire lives not knowing of their existence. But apply the requisite stimulus and there they are in their completeness. ... Whatever their meaning, they forbid our premature closing of our accounts with reality."

So I would say that awakening is the recognition that there are many planes of consciousness and that you exist on all of them. You are limiting yourself incredibly to define yourself only in terms of the physical/psychological planes, as if they were absolutely real. So it's an awakening into the relative reality of the world [that] you thought was absolutely real. It's awakening to realize that you're in a prison you've created by your own thoughts -- that your conceptual definitions of reality are imprisoning you from what reality is, which is something that has no concept. You've reduced yourself into a shadow of who you are, in a reductionistic way, through clinging to concepts, instead of understanding that the true nature of being is not knowing you know, it's simply being.

We get trapped in separateness. When we awaken we realize there's a spiritual dimension to life, that there is a wisdom that lies within the mystery that surrounds life. The answer is that there is something else going on, and realizing this is awakening.[5]

The Danger of the Ultimate Experience

As attractive as awakening may sound and as fundamental as it is to one's finding purpose and meaning in human existence we need to know that not all initiation is pleasant, not all awakening is to joy, and that some initiatory experiences are not only dangerous but can be deadly. Some of the adolescents who were in initiated in the rituals of primitive tribes, after all, died in the process.

Closer to home and more probable is the fact that some of these initiatory and awakening experiences can cause one to lose one's way, to become trapped in deeper illusion, off-balanced, and deceived. It is for this reason that many societies favor the Black-painted approach to spiritual advancement, lest the student wander into self-delusion. Messianic figures, such as Jim Jones with his Peoples' Temple in Guyana, are an extreme example of personal revelation run amok.

Ordinarily, the vital energy serves the common obscure or half-conscious movements of the human mind and human life, its normal ideas, interests, passions and desires. But it is possible for the vital energy to increase beyond the ordinary limits and, if so increased, it can attain an impetus, an intensity, an excitation or sublimation of its forces by which it can become, is almost bound to become an instrument either of divine powers, the powers of the gods, or of Asuric [demoniacal] forces. Or, if there is no settled central control in the nature, its action can be a confused mixture of these opposites, or in an inconsequent oscillation serve now one and now the other. It is not enough then to have a great vital energy acting in you; it must be put in contact with the higher consciousness, it must be surrendered to the true control, it must be placed under the government of the Divine. That is why there is sometimes felt a contempt for the action of the vital force or a condemnation of it, because it has an insufficient light and control and is wedded to an ignorant un-divine movement.[6]

This is not, of course, to dissuade one from seeking progress to spiritual understanding but to remind you that such progress needs to be holistic, not merely based on emotion or perception but on reason and right acting. There is in every thought and action the need for discernment and a clear knowing that the movement and its accompanying realization are consistent with the morality and ethic found in the heart of the authentic self.

Reflecting on Philosophy In the Dungeon

How have you experienced initiation in your life? Can you describe moments of awakening? Can you write about them? How have they affected you for better or for worse? Do you see yourself as evolving? If so in what way would you like to evolve further?

How has your sexual life changed over the years? What kind of initiations have you had sexually? How and when have you awakened sexually? Was this only as an adolescent? When have you awakened at other times and what did you learn in that process?

1   *Gay Soul*, page 186.

2   Cahill, Sedonia & Joshua Halpern, *The Ceremonial Circle*, HarperSanFrancisco, 1990, page 9.

3   Eliade, Mircea, Translated from the French by Willard R. Trask, *Rites and Symbols of Initiation*, Harper & Row, New York, 1958, page 101.

4   *Gay Soul*, pages 158-159.

5   *Gay Soul*, pages 165-166.

6   *The Riddle of This World*, page 18.

Chapter 9

According
to Your Faith

Some dozen or so years ago I visited my godmother, who pulled out some old pictures of our family. In a photo of my parents, my brother, and me, I stood apart, with an awkward stance, and looking rather depressed, especially when compared with my brother who had a big smile on his face. It was a shocker for me to see it, as it showed a side of my childhood that I had hardly remembered.

Before this happened I had thought that my childhood was happy. It was only upon later reflection that I began to remember that I had felt a good deal of rejection in it. I had had rheumatic fever at age ten and so was limited in all the "guy" things I could do. I was a skinny kid with buck teeth and just didn't seem to fit in with the healthy, athletic, and popular boys at St Pius X Elementary School.

With this reflection on that old photograph, I began to see myself as I really had been. I had a deeply hidden self-image of myself as that awkward boy, who was never accepted and always left out. In short I felt that I was a loser. Of course by then I was divorced, estranged from my children, on my parents' list of unapproved people, in deep financial trouble, without a partner, failing to meet my sales quota at work, and generally struggling to get by. My present life hardly looks like that now.

As I wrote in the last chapter, I had been going through a very long depression and was in therapy, trying to figure out what was wrong with me. Today I'm not sure anything was "wrong." Instead I look upon those years as a time of very difficult transition, akin to radical surgery, that would transform my life. Indeed, I hardly recognize the kid in the photo as compared to the adult I am today.

I am at a healthy weight and braces have straightened my teeth. I have two devoted and slavish partners. My finances are manageable and I have a successful writing career, many good friends, and a lifestyle that is genuinely enviable. I would add that my self-image is greatly different and very much improved.

Now one can certainly argue about which comes first: the positive self-image aiding the success or the success creating a positive self-image. This is nothing less than a chicken and egg conundrum, but the fact is that I now have both.

Self-image is the key. How we perceive ourselves and the abilities, talents, and possibilities that we see in our lives directly affect what we do, what risks we take, and how we live. Successful people, after all, believe in themselves; that is to say that they believe in their ability to accomplish their goals and they work to achieve that which they want. Rather than be defeated by their failures they have faith that failure leads to success.

What is important here is self-knowledge, specifically the quality of our knowledge of our self. Though he is specifically speaking of "gay soul" and the anger that is often present within it, an interview with Richard A. Isay, found in *Gay Soul* by Mark Thompson, illustrates my point. Note, too, how understanding ourselves and admitting to our authentic selves, in this case by "coming out," releases the power of our souls:

> We have to know what is inside of ourselves and why it is there. We should understand and nurture the feelings that our anger unleashes so that we can use them in constructive and not self-destructive ways. If we don't know about our disappointments,

frustrations, and injuries, the tendency is to direct our anger in self-destructive ways. I can live with all kinds of terrible feelings. The feelings that injure me are the ones I don't know about.[1]

I would argue that a positive self-image is the most important image to have. Over and over again I am struck by the fact that those who are stuck in a rut greatly fear failure, avoid risk as much as possible, and often create circumstances for themselves that become self-fulfilling and self-defeating prophecies. They do so because of the low esteem they have of themselves.

Let me give an example. A person seeking a partner can post an ad on the Internet with or without a picture. It is a proven fact that ads with photos have a significantly higher success rate than those without. Still there are many ads without a picture because the advertiser doesn't want the exposure a picture will entail. That is their prerogative but by choosing that route, they are causing themselves to be less successful. Having chosen to avoid the problem of exposure, they create the problem of a less-than-successful ad.

If you analyze why one would take a less-successful route there are lots of reasons, such as fear of being outed, possible loss of employment, discovery by one's significant other, the feeling that one's looks are a detriment, etc. In each case the fear of a negative result in itself can become the cause of a negative result.

We do similar things all the time. I remember, for instance, being too depressed to pay my bills, which meant that credit card companies got on my tail, making me more depressed. The reality of the situation was different than my depression would admit. In fact, I had enough money to pay my bills if I just got out of my funk long enough to look at the balance in my checkbook.

I suppose that self-defeating activity is rather common. How many of us don't approach a potential play partner because we fear his or her saying "No?" Our assumption of rejection leads us to eliminate ourselves from consideration, thereby foregoing introducing ourselves, and therefore never giving the other person an opportunity to say "Yes." It is a self-created rejection.

The self-image dilemma has no easy solution, yet solving it in one's life produces a tremendous freedom and increases one's ability to become what one really is. I find myself using the word "authentic" a great deal these days. The challenge we all face is to know our authentic self and then to find the courage to live that authenticity.

Living the authentic self is no easy proposition. Since the earliest days of our childhood we have been socialized to live according to the expectations and requirements of others. Parents are, after all, highly prone to project their dreams onto the lives of their children, filling them with hopes, aspirations, and ideas that conform to what the parents want for their children rather than what might be more authentic to their child's self.

My parents raised me to be Catholic, heterosexual, and a respectable member of American society. While trying to conform to their aspirations for me, I found that my authentic self wanted to live otherwise. For the first thirty-some years of my life, I was either oblivious to the possibility of being other or struggled to repress and deny it. Rather than "To thine (namely my) own self be true," I agonized over being true to the picture my parents (and everyone else) wanted to paint of me.

Yes, I did most of what was expected of me. In fact I did well in school, participated in church as expected, usually did what I was told, and believed that living the life I was presented would make me happy.

It was only when the struggle to be who they wanted had nearly exhausted me that I began to see that I might be happier as someone else. Making that transformation was no easy matter. As I began to succeed in living the life of my real self, my mother would say "We didn't raise you that way," since I was finally living my life, not the one she wanted for me. It was then that I knew I had found myself and that was a good thing. The dire predictions of an early death, of complete rejection, and of "going to Hell," morphed into the real joy of being myself, of knowing that I was finally authentic, of being to my own self true.

Of course, being true to oneself means that one knows oneself. It means that we see ourselves not as we are labeled (and often we label ourselves) but as we are. It also means that we can distinguish between others' projections of ourselves and the true sight of seeing not an image on a screen but the substantial and real individual we are. It means that we begin to understand which voices are old tapes made to conform us to others' expectations and the true voice of our inner self.

What in your knowledge of yourself is the truth and what is merely a projected image? Is your self-image an image of yourself or of the self willed by others? Is the inner voice you hear that of your authentic self or is it merely the echo of a society, a church, or a family that wants you to conform to their estimation of what is right for you? The answers to those questions make a world's difference in one's life and are questions only you can answer.

I'd like to suggest right here that you make a note to come back to these questions and make an attempt at answering them, though the answers may take a lot longer than you expect.

Belief & BDSM

I am left with the question about what does all this have to do with Leather? Our primary concern, after all, is to have fun, not to treat what it is that we do as some kind of therapeutic effort. In fact I can be easily quoted as saying that the dungeon is not an appropriate place for therapy. Leathersex is first about pleasure. If it's not fun, then don't do it.

That written, there is nothing that says that there has to be only one reason to do something. We eat for nourishment (calories,   137 vitamins, and the rest), for pleasure (I hope it tastes good), and for fellowship (who really likes to eat alone, after all?). It's the same with sex, which is meant to do more than just make babies, in spite of what some celibate authorities might want us to think.

Whereas I don't think we should look upon kinky sex as therapy, it most certainly can be therapeutic, especially when it comes to improving one's self image. BDSM can be a healthy outlet for release of tension. It can be an affirming experience of one's strength. It can show us that we are capable. Good scenes improve our self-image, build stronger relationships, and give us a sense of both acceptance and inclusion. This process happens in many ways. It is also a necessary component of healthy SM. Let's look at some of those ways.

First off, our lifestyle, scenes, events, or kinky practices (take your choice here as to what you want to call what it is that you do) place us in the position of having to know what it is that we want to do and/or be. It's not the only activity that makes us think about who we are but it is certainly one that pushes a lot of "who are we" buttons. Are we aggressive or passive? Are we sadistic or masochistic? Are we serious or superficial? Are we in it for the excitement of the moment or the gratification of a long term relationship?

Leather challenges a great many of our assumptions about pain and pleasure, about morality, relationships, integrity, fetish and taboo, sexuality and sexual orientation, and about power and authority. None of this may be immediately apparent when we walk into our first leather bar or join our first kinky newsgroup. Initially we find that kinky sex is about partying and playing.

This finding doesn't last long as we are soon asked what would we like to do. Even the most novice among us has to figure out the answer to that question as well as learn and use good negotiation skills, lest we end up somewhere that we would find very undesirable. Negotiation automatically demands that we know what we want to negotiate, to understand the objectives that we are seeking.

Happily, early negotiations are usually about easy things, such as flogging or getting flogged or bondage or role playing, etc. We therefore cut our teeth on easier questions of identity, a process that then teaches us what we like and don't like. Some of my earliest scenes, for instance, involved urethral sounds and electricity. I learned that neither of those things really turned me on. Other scenes, such as fisting and spanking, did. Voilá. I now knew more about myself without hardly trying. My self image came into a slightly better, clearer focus. This is the way the process usually works and is why we can hardly keep self-images out of the dungeon.

The experience of SM not only teaches us about our likes and dislikes but also demonstrates our strengths. In my own life two examples come easily to mind. In the first case, I never thought of myself as being very strong. As a kid I had rheumatic fever and was under doctor's orders to avoid strenuous exercise. That cut me out of sports, Cub Scouts' hikes, and a host of childhood activities that would have made me "one of the guys." All this fostered a self-image of weakness.

More than twenty years later, my entrance into a leather bar introduced me to "rough sex." I was gently confronted, then, with the question as to whether I was "strong enough" to take a spanking. The wisdom of the day insisted that I had to get before I could give. The Old Guard adage that "Only the best bottoms make it to the top" was in full force. Most everyone was expected to start at the bottom, whether they wanted to or not. Happily tops knew how to handle neophytes like me.

It was a revelation to me that I could take a spanking without making a fool of myself. I was "strong" enough to withstand strap and paddle. I found out what pride a black and blue ass could add to my feelings about who I was and what I was capable of receiving. When I "took it like a man," the taking confirmed my manhood to myself, building and solidifying my self-image in a positive way. It took only a few scenes on someone's lap, for instance, to prove to myself that the playground taunts of my childhood were a thing of the past.

A similar thing happened during my first year as an "out" leatherman. After one particular hot scene with an attractive bartender who had taken a liking to me, he remarked what an excellent top I was. Talk about a boost to one's ego. In one evening I got more positive strokes than in eight years of elementary school. I have to admit it felt good.

Those strokes came often enough from the folks in this new lifestyle that I had to eventually come to the conclusion that they were probably right and that my then poor self-image was most likely inaccurate. It was neither a swift nor easy transformation, but it did occur.

What does all this teach us leather folk? First that we need to know what we want and secondly that Leather presents innumerable opportunities for us to learn about our bodies, our thoughts, and our feelings. Leather creates a unique opportunity for us to experiment and explore, outside the bounds of usual acceptability, free from many of the mores and taboos that bring conformity and stagnation.

As I did with those sounds and that electrical play, we can safely test the waters to see what is authentic to ourselves, and try out new ways of being, doing, and thinking, within the safety net of safe, sane, and consensual. As a microcosm of the world, Leather reflects both the good, the bad, and the ugly. It allows us to experiment without commitment, to see if trying it proves that we like it, and gives us an incredible place to think and act outside the box.

Unlike elementary students, most Leather folk are generally more tolerant, our spaces more accepting, and the possibilities more varied. It's not a perfect place by any means, but certainly one where we can grow and learn, even while we have fun. Who says it has to be either/or? I don't. I want it all --- and we can come close to it!

Belief

Faith and doubt are two sides of the same coin, which is belief. Let me take a moment to use my dictionary to define the terms. Faith is "firm belief in something for which there is no proof;" doubt is "an inclination not to believe or accept;" and belief is "a state or habit of mind in which trust or confidence is placed in some person or thing; conviction of the truth of some statement or reality of fact, especially when well grounded."

Inasmuch as spirituality is based on information arrived at in ways other than the scientific method (i.e., empirical, repeated observation of things and events), it is based on faith. This does, of course, miss the point that one must "believe" in the scientific method, but I don't know that such an argument is germane right now. What is germane is that faith is the underlying basis of perception, action, and creation.

After all, do you remember that tree I saw out my window? I believe I saw it and I would guess that you believe I saw it as well. We will act in a certain way because we believe that doing so will accomplish a certain goal. Less accepted is the idea that we create according to our faith, that our beliefs determine the outcomes of living, as Jesus is quoted in the New Testament, "Let it be done to you according to your faith."

Let us look at some New Testament examples of faith, especially at Jesus' response to the faith of others.[2]

> And behold, a woman who had suffered
> from a hemorrhage for twelve years came up behind
> him and touched the fringe of his garment; for she
> said to herself, "If I only touch his garment, I shall
> be made well." Jesus turned, and seeing her he said,
> "Take heart, daughter; your faith has made you well."

141

And instantly the woman was made well. (Matt 9:22)

This story is recounted in both Mark and Luke, as well:

> And he said to her, "Daughter, your faith
> has made you well; go in peace, and be healed of your
> disease." (Mark 5:34)

And he said to her, "Daughter your faith has made you well; go in peace." (Luke 8:48)

And again:

> And as Jesus passed on from there, two
> blind men followed him, crying aloud, "Have mercy
> on us, Son of David." When he entered the house, the
> blind men came to him and Jesus said to them, "Do
> you believe that I am able to do this?" They said to
> him, "Yes, Lord." Then he touched their eyes, saying,
> "According to your faith be it done to you." And their
> eyes were opened. (Matt 9:29)

> And Jesus said to him, "What do you want
> me to do for you?" And the blind man said to him,
> "Master, let me receive my sight." And Jesus said to
> him, "Go your way; your faith has made you well."
> And immediately he received his sight and followed
> him on the way. (Mark 10:52)

It is interesting that in this next story it is the faith of his friends that healed that paralytic:

> And behold, they brought to him a paralytic,
> lying on his bed; and when Jesus saw their faith he
> said to the paralytic, "Take heart, my son; your sins
> are forgiven." And behold, some of the scribes said
> to themselves, "This man is blaspheming." But Jesus,

knowing their thoughts, said, "Why do you think evil in your hearts? For which is easier, to say, 'Your sins are forgiven,' or to say, 'Rise and walk'? But that you may know that the Son of man has authority on earth to forgive sins" -- he then said to the paralytic -- "Rise, take up your bed and go home." And he rose and went home. When the crowds saw it, they were afraid, and they glorified God, who had given such authority to men. (Matt 9:2-8)

And in Mark we can read the same:

> And when Jesus saw their faith, he said to the paralytic, "My son, your sins are forgiven." (Mark 2:5)

> And behold, a Canaanite woman from that region came out and cried, "Have mercy on me, O Lord, Son of David; my daughter is severely possessed by a demon."... Then Jesus answered her "O woman, great is your faith! Be it done for you as you desire." And her daughter was healed instantly. Matt 15:22 & 28)

And finally:

> And behold, a woman of the city, who was a sinner... And he said to the woman, "Your faith has saved you; go in peace." (Luke 7:37 & 50)

Most Christians consistently interpret these passages as proof of the value of placing one's faith in Jesus. I propose that this is a natural interpretation only when one makes a superficial evaluation of the texts. Reading the texts more closely it is obvious that in each case, Jesus notes that it is faith that has caused the cure, not him. In none of these passages does he say anything like "Your faith in me has cured you."

143

Note that it doesn't even take one's own faith to cause a healing, as the paralytic was healed not by his faith, but by the faith of his friends. The text is clear: "when Jesus saw their faith" he forgave the paralytic's sins. The possessive pronoun "their" refers to them, not the paralytic.

Faith

Too often, we understand the word faith as applying to one's set of religious beliefs, especially when we are talking about spirituality. Just as I don't want to think of spirituality as separate from the rest of one's life, so too faith cannot be set apart. We live our lives according to our faith. We believe that a bridge is safe, so we cross it. We believe attendance at a certain school will help educate us, so we go there. We believe vitamins are good for us; tobacco is not, that a particular action will bring us pleasure, that another one will put us in jail.

This is the pervasiveness of faith. Whether one is religious or not, atheistic or not, even believing or not, since even not believing is a form of faith in that it is faith in the opposite. To say "I don't believe in God" is to say that "I believe in not-God."

Even our self-image is directly linked to our faith. A positive self-image is, after all, one that believes in oneself, while a negative one is fraught with self-doubt, with unbelief in oneself.

This is to say, then, that every action is based on some kind or degree of faith or non-faith (doubt) so that "According to your faith" means that as you believe so you will live, create, and be.

Manifestation

Before I discuss the implications of faith, let me attempt to define that which faith produces, namely manifestation. My dictionary defines it in this way: "the act, process, or an instance of manifesting; something that manifests; one of the forms in which an individual is manifested; an occult phenomenon, specifically materialization; a public demonstration of power and purpose." To manifest is "to make evident or certain by showing or displaying."

> Every effect we produce by thought, word, or deed is a manifestation that naturally flows from and is produced by those thoughts, words, and deeds. Though we tend to use the word manifestation in circumstances that are more akin to demonstrations of power, I contend that we manifest all the time, that every action is a manifestation. It is not an occult phenomenon but it is a public demonstration of power and purpose. Manifestation is simply the effect of natural law.

Some manifestations are called occult or miraculous only because the one who names them as such doesn't understand the underlying principles that naturally and always cause that effect. It is, then, simply a matter of cause and effect, hence

Your faith determines what you manifest.

Now if we take that statement simplistically we are going to get into a lot of trouble, as I will explain later. We cannot look at faith as the sole determinative of manifestation because manifestation is affected by other forces as well, which is to say that an effect may, and usually does, have many causes.

Too often we understand "having faith" as a passive undertaking or as believing in a set of dogmas or principles or ideas. Faith thus becomes an intellectual activity. The fact is, I believe, that faith that is only ideation, only thought, has little or no power. Faith is rather part of the manifestation equation. It is only one of the determining forces. The other is power, the ability to effect change.

There is a bit of a tautology here that needs to be noted, 145 as faith in itself is a form of power. Here, though, it is the directing power rather than the effecting power. Take the example of a very wealthy child who is separated from his family at an early age and is entirely unaware of his large inheritance -- sort of a Harry Potter type. Though he has the power of his riches, his ignorance of it leaves him powerless to use it in his life. The fact that he believes he is poor directs his actions accordingly. Now, on the other hand, if he were to discover his true heritage, and claim his inheritance, his faith in his wealth and his power to use it would change his life.

This power to act comes in a great many forms: speech, movement, thought, acting, doing, giving, keeping, receiving, and so forth. Let me illustrate with the story of the manifestation of a house.

Two people, a couple living together in an apartment, are talking one night over dinner and the conversation turns to housing. They want their own home. This is the beginning. Over the next few weeks they discuss what kind of home and where; they read the home section of their local newspapers to clarify their thinking. They go looking at homes that are for sale and decide they want one built to their specifications. Excitedly they begin drawing floor plans and collecting pictures of housing details that they want.

In another few weeks or so, they believe they know what their new house should look like and they believe that they can afford it. They have faith and they've put some energy -- in the form of time, travel, looking, talking, thinking, planning, and researching -- into making that which they want real, i.e., manifested.

So they hunt up an architect who takes their idea and adds his power: time, drafting, calculating, etc. The couple are also now adding more energy, in the form of money, to their faith. You see, they could believe all they wanted to that an architect could draw plans; the architect's faith in his need to be paid for his services affects the outcome as well.

146

They find a parcel of land upon which to build their home. Now the banker will add his faith in the couple's ability to pay the mortgage and his faith in his own ability to have the necessary funds to pay the contractor, whom the couple will hire because they believe he will do a good job following the architect's plans which they believe will cause their dream house to be built as they want it. Not to belabor the point, but the contractor will add the energy of wood, glass, shingles, cement, plaster, paint, wiring, appliances, more time, and lots of carpentry, electrical, and plumbing energy to manifest, i.e., build, this house.

The power that joins with faith to create is known by many names, a good number of which don't even seem to refer to "power" per se. Think passion, drive, enthusiasm, perseverance, desire, effort, stubbornness, money, time, skill, daring, boldness, hope, resignation, repetition, and all the myriad feelings (both positive and negative) and desires that motivate, energize, and compel human life.

It is not always an easy path to manifestation, especially when the kind of faith that directs our energy is often doubting and fearful. Having the faith necessary to do something often involves pain and suffering. I am mindful of the answer my grandmother Santa gave when asked what my great-grandfather said as she left him to join her husband in America. My grandparents came to America because they had faith that they would find a better life for themselves and their children. Even with such a faith, my grandmother heard her father say "Today you are dying to me and that ship is your coffin. I will never see you again."

Faith needs what my grandparents had as they left all they knew for a new life: courage.

"According to your faith," then, is not a matter of simple hocus pocus, especially since faith is a matter of not only what a person thinks or says he or she believes, but rather of what and how one really believes.

I, for instance, once believed that I could establish and

manage my own publishing company. In 1986 I started one. I had no idea of the tremendous undertaking into which I was entering. My faith in my entrepreneurial talents might have been OK, but it was sorely tempered by my financial doubts, my ever-deepening depression, and my inability to distinguish between what I believed and what I hoped. The fact that some few loving friends believed in me enough to lend me money was offset by the doubt of many who declined to be involved. Five years of labor and angst left me nearly bankrupt. It was a costly education and a publishing failure -- as the friends and the authors who believed in me will attest.

Nearly twenty years later I successfully published my own book. Again my friends, more than 300 of them, helped and no one lost anything. My faith had developed, my knowledge had increased, my power had grown. Even the failure of the first attempt was part of the manifestation of the successful try as that first failure contained important lessons for my future success. In each case, the formula was the same: Faith plus power equals manifestation or, in other words, it is done according to your faith.

Reflecting on Philosophy In the Dungeon

We too often think that only saints and those who live in monasteries are men and women of faith. What faith did Columbus have to sail west from Spain or Isabella to sell her jewels to finance his trip? What faith did the Pilgrims have to leave the comfort of Holland for the wilds of the New World? Or Marconi to build the first radio or Edison to persevere through more than a thousand failed attempts to invent the light bulb?

Faith, you see, is not a matter of simply "Believe on the Lord Jesus Christ and you shall be saved" but rather "Let it be done to you according to your faith."

More often than not one's faith sheds negativity on our sexuality activities -- the taboos against masturbation, premarital sex, and same-sex relationships are only the tip of that

148

devastatingly cold iceberg. Sexual organs are more often seen as dirty than sacred; sexual activity as immoral rather than uplifting. It is high time for a new paradigm for our understanding of sex, or perhaps to revive some old ones, to rid sex of its veil of guilt and shame, to restore it to its natural glory, sacredness, and holiness.

What do you believe and why? How does your faith enliven and enrich or handicap and kill your sexual life?

1   *Gay Soul*, page 41.
2   The following quotes are all taken from the Harper Study Bible, *Revised Standard Version*.

Chapter 10

True Spirituality

T he last chapter, I hope, is an enthusiastic essay to inspire you to believe. We are, I am sure, meant to live a life of faith. In fact we probably don't have much choice in that, as all of us have to believe someone or something more often than not.

On the other hand, it is important that we take a deep breath and understand what that means. There are many faiths reflecting a wide variety of spiritualities in the world and they are not all as helpful as we might wish. (Here I also count the spiritualities of those who say they have no need of spirit nor a belief in such things.) The deep breath is meant to give us a moment to reflect and center ourselves, to remember to keep our balance.

If nothing else, true spirituality, an authentic manifestation of holiness, that which is whole, is balanced. I learned that lesson the scary way.

I spent the years between 1965 and '69 studying for the priesthood. Part of that training, of course, was spent in prayer, either at Mass, chanting Psalms, or reflecting and meditating. While experiencing the inner workings of a seminary and considering the priesthood as a lifetime commitment, I was struck by the difference between twentieth-century Catholicism and Christianity as seen through the words one reads in the Acts of the Apostles.

Silver and gold have I none; but such as
I have give I thee: In the name of Jesus Christ of

Nazareth rise up and walk. And he took him by the
right hand, and lifted him up: and immediately his feet
and ankle bones received strength. And he leaping
up stood, and walked, and entered with them into the
temple, walking, and leaping, and praising God. (Acts
4:6-8)

I saw the Roman Catholic Church as wealthy in material
goods but often bereft of the miraculous power of faith. Thus it
was that I began to pray to be filled with the Holy Spirit as were
Peter and John and the others. The answer to that prayer I have
already described in my receiving the Baptism in the Holy Spirit
in a restaurant on that Saturday morning in 1969. My Pentecostal
experiences eventually led me to join a New Testament community
called Love Inn in Freeville, NY, where I served in several
capacities until those dark nights of the soul ravaged my joy and
caused me to leave that fellowship.

In 1978 Pastor Jim Jones, who had led his followers to
establish a religious commune in Guyana, oversaw their mass
suicide. Love Inn had always managed to stay clear of cult status
and its fundamentalism was never as hard-core as it might have
been -- we never gave up drinking or dancing for instance, nor
handled snakes or drank poison -- but there were clear similarities
between the believers at Jonesville and those in Freeville. I
was struck by the realization that, but for the grace of God, we
could have ended up with the same fate. The men and women of
Jonesville, together with their unsuspecting children, had moved
far away from the center of healthy living and a real spiritual life.
They had lost their balance.

It was that shocking realization of the dnager of
fundamentalism and its ensuing loss of balance, that led me to pray
for and to try to live a balanced life.

Faith is just one way of knowing and only part of the
creating and manifesting process. As a form of knowing, it is

152

a belief in that which is not otherwise presently verifiable. A balanced faith recognizes that there are many ways to know, and allows as full a knowledge as possible to be the basis of knowledge in general and action in particular.

A city can be described in many ways: by its population, its layout, its architecture, its location, its commerce, etc. No one way of looking at a city accurately describes it all. Each way we perceive it adds another perspective, a new dimension, and a vitality not found otherwise. A city is also more than the sum of its parts. It is an interconnected unity of grids upon grids. A city's inner connectivity is seen in its electrical grid, its telephone lines and cables, its roads, its sewers and water pipes; in its political, familial, neighborly, and commercial relationships. It is a unity that can be known in so many ways that we don't even perceive all of them.

So it is that faith adds an important dimension to our knowing, but is not the only dimension. To remain healthy our knowledge must also be experiential, emotional, intellectual, rational, scientific, intuitive, and more. In short, full knowledge comes through many ways of knowing and our faith must remain one part, as best we can make it, but not the only part of our knowing.

It is the same with our creating and manifesting. Just believing that something will come to pass will not make it so. Our lives are composites of all that make us who and what we are. Faith is an important element but, again, not the only element. We are just as much a "product" of physics, biology, history, and linguistics as we are of faith and belief, of dogma and doctrine.

Present-day America, and indeed the world as a whole, has witnessed a resurgence of unbalanced religious fundamentalism, a literalist and generally intolerant understanding of some of the basic doctrines of the great teachers. So the Hasidim adhere to Moses, conservative Evangelicals to Jesus, the Al Qaeda to Mohamed. Their message is that salvation, the attainment of heaven, is based on a faith-only path, on what appears to be a blind obedience to the letter of the law, especially one that believes that their way is the ONLY way.

That's not to say that fundamentalist sects are anything new. Literal, puritanical, and fanatical religious interpretations have been around much longer than we can imagine. There is nothing new about religious wars, inquisitions, and persecutions. Few, if any, religious groups can claim to have been entirely innocent in this regard. If anything the religions of the world have shown a greater love for self-righteousness than for being right, and for intolerance rather than for loving their enemies.

I am not opposed to a message of salvation. I write this only as a preface to the idea that those who preach salvation do their believers a disservice if they do not also teach them to live a balanced and virtuous life.

Why is this? The answer depends upon the doctrine of the Faith in question, of course, but what the great faiths have in common is a code of justice and morality that is based on living a virtuous life. Coming from the Latin "virtus" meaning strength, manliness, virtue, and derived from the root word *vir*, meaning man, virtue means "Conformity to a standard of right; a particular moral excellence" and as such it leads to a lifestyle wherein one is authentic to him- or herself and respectful of the authenticity of his fellow humans and the environment in which he finds himself. In all of this, virtue requires a balance between self and others, a centered approach that considers one's whole being.

Knowing Oneself

To live in this fashion, to be authentic, means that we need first to know the authentic self, to probe deeply into our self-ness in order to be aware of who we really are. Knowing oneself is 154 a life-long process as the self that one knows is continually faced with life-changing experiences and so grows and matures. Every experience, after all, is life-changing in some way. Even walking down the street changes our position in the universe!

The soul, then, brings us experiences that have the potential of revealing our self to our self, if we are willing to listen. Having heard, we then know who we are and how to proceed. Doing so may not be an easy proposition as we are deluged with other ideas and other forces that would have us live lives that conform to others' projections and aspirations of who we should be. It takes courage to be oneself in the face of others' expectations. Still, living an authentic life is the path that leads to true power.

Motivation

The sheer complexities of human life and living compound the search for self-knowledge in what often seems to be an infinite number of ways. In an attempt to understand myself and as an aid to understanding others, I suggest that we look at our motivations as an appropriate guide. That's not to say that motivation is the only criterion for evaluation, since even the best intentions can go awry, can lead one astray. On the other hand, "Everyone has an agenda." Knowing our agenda helps to bring clarity to the relationship, whether it be long term, romantic, financial, bureaucratic, sexual, or political, to mention but a view of the places where motivation matters.

Each action is begun and sustained by one's motivation for that action, so to consider all motivations and all actions is a rather hopeless undertaking. Instead, an overview of all our actions can lead to an understanding of one's primary motivations. In reality we consciously and (more often) unconsciously evaluate all actions by what motivates us, giving priority to stronger and more basic motives while trying to accommodate less important and less critical motivations.

Abraham Maslow's work in analyzing and understanding

motivations, which he called needs, led to his famous Pyramid of Needs as seen in illustration four. Understanding from whence we function in terms of these needs is an important way to understand ourselves. If we are, for instance, still struggling for physiological satisfaction, namely that we are hungry, homeless, and at our wits' ends in trying to survive, then other needs are going to be far less important.

Maslow also recognized that some needs remain subconsciously salient, even when outwardly they seem to have been satisfied. So it is, for instance, that an adult who suffered financial deprivation as a child might never know true financial

Being Needs

Self-Actualization

Esteem Needs

Belonging Needs

Deficit Needs

Safety Needs

Physiological Needs

Illustration Four[1]

security. His or her need for financial strength, even under the circumstances of plenty, may always be a strong, if not the strongest, motivator.

Recognizing one's place on Maslow's pyramid helps us to understand why we act in certain ways and therefore is an aid to acting differently. If we know, for instance, that we have a strong, deep seated need to belong, we can then understand that we will do much for acceptance, even if doing so might lower our self-esteem or hinder the satisfaction of our physiological needs. As an example, one might undergo a humiliating initiation in order to join a fraternity and that initiation might put one's safety at risk. Still, our belonging need in this situation exercises strong control over our behavior. On the other hand, we might choose our need for self-esteem or a sense of safety and drop out of the initiation.

What then motivates you? Why are you kinky? Why are you a member of a BDSM organization (or not as the case might be)? Why are you submissive or dominant? Sadistic or masochistic? Why are you reading this book?

One of the purposes of understanding our motivations is that we can then understand and direct our behavior in appropriate ways. Though it's not as if our actions are always based on reason, it is probably helpful that they be reasonable. We usually have a multitude of reasons for doing something. Our decisions are seldom only reasonable. In fact, emotions, finances, morality, time, ability, circumstances, and each of the needs broadly outlined by Maslow influence many of our decisions, even when we fail to note that we are making a decision.

Mystical Experience

There are, as I hope I've made clear, a great many ways to arrive at one's spirituality. I hold the place of experience high in this process, though I will be quick to add that experience alone is not a solid foundation for faith, since even experience can be deceptive or at least perceived in a less-than-actual way. It is the same with mystical experience. Though there is information to be gained in the experience of an awakening, of a white light, or of a dramatic vision, even these events need be balanced by a holistic approach to knowing.

On the other hand, a spirituality devoid of mystical

experience probably leaves something to be desired or at least leaves some "'rocks unturned" in its quest for truth. To base all our knowing on empirical evidence, to refuse to open oneself to the infinities of possibilities, to box oneself into a corner that allows only for information that comes through one's five senses is to limit oneself and deny one's greater potential. Mystical experience, as well as many other non-linear, non-physical modes of knowing, is just as appropriate a way to learn as is the scientific method. Mystical experience is in fact another kind of process. Let me quote Andrew Harvey:

What do you mean by mystical process?

I mean by the word mystical entering into conscious direct relationship with the divine. It must be conscious and it must be direct to be mystical. Mystical is not theological; it's not having a series of ideas about God, however lucid or wonderful. It's not emotional; it's not having a series of feelings, however deep and adoring, about God. And it's not intellectual, in any sense, even in the most refined sense.

What it means is having direct contact in the soul, the core of being, with the Source. That can take place in many different ways, but its primary ways are through an opening of what people call the third eye. Through devotion, mystical prayer, and the saying of mantras, all the senses of the subtle body -- the spiritual senses, if you like -- wake up and begin to see and interpret the world in a completely fresh way.

The world remains the same but appears now drenched in light and transparent and is experienced far more like a magical film than as something inherently real. The ego stops interpreting and deforming, and you begin to see the primal, divine world in its pain and beauty and to respond to it with the love of the soul, which is one with the love that creates all things.[2]

158

Here we find one of the fundamental differences between spiritualities of the West and those of the East. Western religions, especially Christianity, teach that faith must precede experience, as in "Believe and ye shall be saved." Faith comes first. In the East it is more the case of the opposite -- do these things to have these experiences and then you will know and your faith will grow.

In some ways this is a chicken and egg argument and I'm not about to tell you which paradigm will work for you. What I will note is that mystical experience can be as valid as physical experience, if one but approaches it holistically.

Up until now I have only mentioned my own mystical experiences. Let me try to describe them further. Before I do so, I would like to add two caveats. First, time has eroded the memory of these events so you'll have to pardon me if I don't have an exact recollection of what happened to me as a ten-or-twelve-year-old. Secondly, my experiences are just that, my experiences. Your own mystical experiences, as well as those of others, will quite probably be significantly different. What will be the same for all of us is the transcendent nature, the experience of realizing Other and of being part of Other.

As I mentioned in the Introduction, my first transcendent encounter with God occurred during my adolescence, somewhere around 1958. I had asked for, and my parents had given me, a Bible for Christmas and since these were the days of Latin Masses and relatively silent Catholic congregations, I took to bringing it to Mass with me and reading it. My intention was to start at the beginning and read it all the way through. Today I'm not sure that I accomplished that feat, though later in life I did.

As far as I can recollect, I put the Bible down to go up to the altar rail to receive communion, walked back to the pew where we were sitting, knelt down, lowered my head, and prayed. As the unleavened bread melted in my mouth (we were taught

159

not to chew it) I felt enveloped in a very comforting, yet very bright, light. For the moment, all was silent. I was surrounded by a majestic, silent, and awesome Reality. I felt total peace and safety. I knew that not only had I received God in the Eucharist but that God had received me.

Though the details are less remembered, I attended a weekend retreat at a monastery during Easter weekend of my Senior year of high school. The weekend was spent in silence, prayer, and listening to talks about the Passion, Death, and Resurrection of Jesus. During a slide show and lecture on the Shroud of Turin, I became impressed with the Love of God for me, not an untypical event given the circumstances. Sometime thereafter, whether on Saturday night during the Easter Vigil Mass or the next morning just prior to leaving the retreat, I was once again overcome by some spiritual presence, so much so that I resolved to enter the priesthood.

When I returned to join my family for Easter dinner, I was filled with joy, bliss, and peace, though I don't remember saying much about it at the time and my resolve to become a priest did not last very long. It was only later in the summer that it returned and I eventually entered the seminary.

Though my seminary days were filled with pleasant and reaffirming glimpses of the divine, it was only after I had left the seminary and begun investigating the promises and teachings of what was then called the Catholic Pentecostal Movement or the Catholic Charismatic Movement, that I had another powerful experience of God. The white light of my adolescent experience during communion was once again present as I attempted to speak in tongues during that Full Gospel Businessmen's Meeting at the restaurant.

I ought to follow that up with the fact that though I did not speak in tongues at the time, while driving to school (I was also attending some summer classes that year) I began to utter a strange language. Subsequently, as I became more involved in Pentecostalism, many of those New Testament "gifts" were manifested in my life, including Prophecy and the Interpretation of Tongues.

This experience led me to become an active part-time evangelist in the Northeast and then to join the Love Inn community on a full-time basis. I've already recounted my experiences after that, which led to my divorce and my participation in the Gay community of Ft. Wayne, Indiana.

By 1985 I had developed a Master/slave relationship with Steve, my partner at the time. It was an experiment for both of us, as we explored what it meant to be kinky, dominant/submissive Leather men. One weekend evening we were playing in my small apartment. I remember that we were both naked and that I had given Steve an enema. As he sat on the toilet, I hovered over him playing with his genitals and his anus. I remember that we were kissing and that I was highly sexually aroused.

I don't remember much else except that all of a sudden I once again felt this Divine presence. Once again I felt surrounded by a bright white light, by an extraordinary sense of peace and joy, and complete safety. Unlike my adolescent experience, this time I knew that Steven was part of the experience, that he must be feeling the same thing.

I'm not sure how long the light lasted. It may have been mere seconds or several minutes. When it passed, I said to Steven "Wow. Did you feel that?" He answered in the affirmative and we quietly cleaned up and went to bed to cuddle and have intercourse.

The last event that I will recount happened while I was in a Master/slave relationship with my good friend Lynn. On this night we were in his basement playroom. By now we had been partnered for over a year and were quite comfortable with each other. I had shared many of my rituals with Lynn and we often began playing by creating a sacred circle (more on this later). Once that was done, we would proceed to have a rather intense sadomasochist scene. I was, in those days, his slave and bottom.

He controlled the direction and the events of the sex and did it quite well.

On this night, I remember that he had flogged and spanked me. I am not sure if I was bound at the time or not, though that was often part of the impact play. In any case I was hooded and therefore blindfolded and I was kneeling on the playroom floor. In this condition I saw a light in the darkness of the hood. It grew into the shape of an eye and then into a face which was obviously watching me.

The face had the appearance of a black and white mask, one quite similar to those made by primitive tribes. It was elongated, painted in the fashion of Indian war paint, and surrounded by wild, unkempt hair. In spite of its appearance it presented me with nothing that I found threatening or fearful. It was a peaceful presence that just seemed to be watching me with curiosity.

Subsequently I have often seen that "eye" during times of meditation and times of sexual bliss. It looks just like the eye on the top of the pyramid on the back of a one dollar bill.

Topspace as a Spiritual Event

Most players with any experience know that there is some kind of spiritual or mystical experience connected with being a bottom. That's why we use the term "subspace" so often. What is less understood is topspace.

Topping is a pathway that allows me to enter an altered (sacred) space that has two aspects. The first is what I might call (coining terms on the fly) the affirmation aspect. The second is that topping is foreplay that increases the intensity of my orgasm which I often use as an entry into a deeper sacred space.

The affirmation space is a feeling of power over my partner. Now this is consensual, given to me through his surrender and my assuming control. I'll have to start this explanation with the note that I primarily play with those willing to submit and surrender, rather than with bottoms who (in my not so humble opinion) maintain control during the scene and are in it primarily for their own pleasure, not mine. I am almost embarrassed to talk about this as, when taken out of context, it may well be seen as an incredible ego trip.

A significant part of this variety of topping is the act of worship. The power given to me by my partner and the control that I therefore legitimately and consensually exercise helps me to recognize my divinity.

In this topping I realize and embrace that I am godly, that I am god. Indeed I begin to feel that I am divine, to sense in my body the power of the universe. Physically I feel actual sensations of energy flow, especially the rising of Kundalini from the sexual center to my head. Sometimes this is the experience of a vibration, at other times of electricity. I would like to note, too, that the most intense experiences are much rarer than the less intense ones, though some of this happens nearly all the time to some degree.

The previous paragraph about my being godly is obviously fraught with danger. The recognition that I am god is in fact the recognition that each and every one of us is god. For only one of us to be god is a betrayal of the truth of our own divinity, and the divinity of all creation in general and humanity in particular. If I, as a human, am godly it is therefore irrefutable that all humans are as well. The slave's worship of me is only the slave's recognition of his or her own divinity. In fact, it is god worshipping god.

Worship of the top-god by the bottom-god uses the energy flow generated to put both into altered states. The conclusion I have come to is that the greater the polarity between the partners, the greater the energy flow. In other words, the more dominant I become and the more surrendered my partner becomes, the greater the polarity and hence the greater the possibility of heightened energy states and therefore deeper, more intense, altered space

163

experiences. It is impossible for the polarities to be unequal. A master cannot, for instance, become more of a master, unless his or her slave is willing to become more slavish. In other words, two things that are distant from one another (polarized) are always the same distance from each other; A is as far from B as B is from A.

As a side note, this is why I have chosen to have multiple slaves. I am wary of the physical/psychological danger of one slave becoming too slavish to one master. The solution is for one master to have two (or more) slaves, therefore becoming more masterful.

Paradoxically, being one slave of two is more slavish than being the only slave, but presents less physical/psychological danger. For example one can only whip a person so much before the scene becomes physically dangerous, but one could whip two slaves in the same scene thereby generating more excitement and energy. It can be just as exciting to whip two slaves as it is to whip one slave twice as hard.

Experiencing my divinity brings me closer to the fundamental reality that I am one with the universe, or what the Hindus would call the Void. I am a manifestation (incarnation) of God and this topspace allows me to experience myself as an incarnation. I think it is noteworthy that in the best of these scenes, not only does my slave worship me but I find that I begin to worship myself.

More than 18 years ago, I realized the very real similarity between deep meditative states and the "glow" that accompanies orgasm. The altered state that both produce is one in which creativity and manifestation become easier to accomplish. Altered states have two purposes above and beyond the experience of pleasure: the first is for action, the second is for learning.

Sex Magic (which will be covered in greater detail later) is all about action, that is entering an altered state to produce some manifestation such as peace, health, harmony, or prosperity, expressed in concrete ways. In that way it is identical to prayer. I have purposely stated two purposes, though the second is actually only another form of manifestation, which is learning.

Being in an altered state of consciousness (at least of the variety of which I am speaking) gives us an experience of and therefore teaches us essential facts about the ground of our being. By experiencing this "universe" we learn what we are made of. We experience the essence of our existence, which is godliness. We learn that we are one with all that is, which means that we are intimately and eternally connected with all.

I have learned ways to remain in this orgasm-induced state for longer than usual, though even at that the state is none too long. Part of this, of course, is that my partners are taught to be very still until I have "returned." This is an interesting phenomenon. I once had a trick who was very freaked out by the fact that after orgasm he thought I had gone comatose and rushed out of the room to ask Patrick's help in reviving me.

The challenge is to take the lessons learned in this altered state and apply them to "normal" living. To do this we must always find ways to stay grounded even as we fly. This altered state ought to have two parts. The Kundalini energy is meant to rise from the sexual center to the transpersonal point (from Earth to Sky) and then return from Sky to Earth, making it fertile and productive, recognizing the fundamental unity of the sacred and the mundane.

Let me return to the polarity discussion. In a very real sense the polarity that is created is that of the Sky Father relating to the Earth Mother. Humans have this wonderful capacity to be the bridge (probably not the only bridges but certainly a real one) between those two divine entities. Rather than there being a conflict between Sky Father (Ouranos) and Earth Mother (Gaia) there is meant to be a union, the fecundity of which is all of creation.

This, I believe, is the essence of the ancient fertility rites and sexually-based worship of cultures such as Sumer and Canaan, unfortunately destroyed by those religions whose notion of a Sky Father (Jehovah) could not tolerate an Earth Mother. In this, of course, one partner takes on the role (the essence?) of one divinity while the other takes on the role of the other. Taking this idea further, partners have the potential of becoming a wide variety of pairs, not only Ouranos and Gaia, but Zeus and Hera, Siva and Sakti or Dionysos and the Maenads.

This is what I think happens when I top. All I can really say about it is that I am still learning and as yet haven't learned much.

Evaluation

The challenge in mystical experience is to evaluate its meaning and impact, to consider its source, its motivation, and the virtue it engenders or hinders. Evaluation demands discernment, "Skill in discerning or discriminating: keenness of insight." To discern is "to see or understand the difference." When we discern, we recognize the source, the motivation, the validity and authenticity of that which we experience. To do so is not always easy, though usually it is quite helpful. Discernment means we remove those rose-colored glasses to the best of our ability, seeing and experiencing that which is before us in a holistic way that can lead to more truth.

Too often, unfortunately, we fail to see correctly, our "vision" clouded by fear, by self-image, by pre-conceived ideas, by our culture, our hang-ups, and our motivations. These hindrances need to be recognized and accounted for and our interpretation of our perceptions adjusted accordingly

Aurobindo wrote about mystical experience that was incorrectly interpreted, calling it experience in the "intermediate zone," that is between mundane life and enlightenment:

For this intermediate zone is a region of
half-truths -- and that by itself would not matter,
for there is no complete truth below the Supermind;

but the half-truth here is often so partial or else ambiguous in its application that it leaves a wide field for confusion, delusion and error. The sadhak [one who is getting or trying to get realization] thinks that he is no longer in the old small consciousness at all, because he feels in contact with something larger or more powerful, and yet the old consciousness is still there, not really abolished. He feels the control or influence of some Power, Being or Force greater than himself, aspires to be its instrument and thinks he has got rid of ego; but this delusion of egolessness often covers an exaggerated ego. Ideas seize upon him and drive his mind which are only partially true and by overconfident misapplication are turned into falsehoods; this vitiates the movements of the consciousness and opens the door to delusion. Suggestions are made, sometimes of a romantic character, which flatter the importance of the sadhak or are agreeable to his wishes and he accepts them without examination or discriminating control. Even what is true, is so exalted or extended beyond its true pitch and limit and measure that it becomes the parent of error. This is a zone which many sadhaks have to cross, in which many wander for a long time and out of which a great many never emerge. Especially if their sadhana is mainly in the mental and vital, they have to meet here many difficulties and much danger; only those who follow scrupulously a strict guidance or have the psychic being prominent in their nature pass easily as if on a sure and clearly marked road across this intermediate region. A central sincerity, a fundamental humility also save from much danger and trouble. One can then pass quickly beyond into a clearer Light where if there is still much mixture, incertitude and struggle, yet the orientation is towards the cosmic Truth and not to a half-illumined prolongation of Maya [the divine power which has created the cosmos] and ignorance.[3]

Ordinarily, the vital energy serves the common obscure or half-conscious movements of the human mind and human life, its normal ideas, interests, passions and desires. But it is possible for the vital energy to increase beyond the ordinary limits and, if so increased, it can attain an impetus, an intensity, an excitation or sublimation of its forces by which it can become, is almost bound to become an instrument either of divine powers, the powers of the gods, or of Asuric [demoniacal] forces. Or, if there is no settled central control in the nature, its action can be a confused mixture of these opposites, or in an inconsequent oscillation serve now one and now the other. It is not enough then to have a great vital energy acting in you; it must be put in contact with the higher consciousness, it must be surrendered to the true control, it must be placed under the government of the Divine. That is why there is sometimes felt a contempt for the action of the vital force or a condemnation of it, because it has an insufficient light and control and is wedded to an ignorant un-divine movement.[4]

The Correct Course

What we are left with then is to find and maintain balance, to live in such a way as to grow in wisdom and knowledge while living a life based on virtue, which directs our actions towards ourselves, others, and our environment. It is more than simply doing good; it is a faithfulness to the self which we know to be authentic. As Will Roscoe notes:

Our service now has to be to the truth of ourselves, to finding what feels right -- if it's a jump rope or whatever it's going to be. Only by doing that can we come to our powers. Politically speaking, what we need from society is protection so that we can have our space, so that we can come to our powers and give them back to the larger community.[5]

And as Aurobindo notes:

> I would have to say, honor yourself. Take
> everything about yourself seriously. Pay attention
> to your desire and where it's taking you. It's all
> significant. But don't take things so seriously that you
> stop having fun. By all means, don't deny yourself
> pleasure.[6]

Too often we are liable to lose our balance because we
focus too directly on one or another preoccupation. Many of us
therefore know family members, friends, and acquaintances who
are workaholics, religious fanatics, or are otherwise so intent
on one aspect of life that the rest of their lives and relationships
suffer. They seem to have become myopic in their vision, narrow,
stagnant, or overboard in one side of life while neglecting other
sides. An extreme loss of balance leads to addiction, obsession,
and the dangerous cultivation of one side to the ruin of others.

Only by remaining holistic in our outlook can we remain
whole. A balanced life is not a luxury. It is a necessity for real
fulfillment and true spirituality.

Reflecting on Philosophy In the Dungeon

It may be more realistic to write that we are never in
balance, or at least seldom so. Rather we swing towards balance
and then away from it, as a pendulum in continual motion. The
answer, of course, is to learn to rest more in that centered space,
which is easier said than done. To give balance to these words of
this chapter, where I come rather harshly down on fundamentalists,
it is only fair to note that a left-wing, anything-goes anarchistic
and materialistic belief structure is just as unbalanced.

The lesson of this chapter is meant for the bedroom and

dungeon as well as in the rest of one's life. In sex, balance is found between the partners, each physically, sexually, energetically in balance with the other. BDSM play, for instance, isn't all sadomasochism but includes moments of tender affection amid the lashes of the whip. Surrender is not entirely and only one to the other, but moves from one to the other as the scene progresses. The partners may be poles apart in one moment and move into the center together in the next.

Even when their play is highly polarized, when they are seen as a bonded couple, together they reflect a unified state in balance, or so one would hope.

1   Adapted from Boeree, C. George, *Abraham Maslow*, found at http://www.ship.edu/~cgboeree/maslow.html on January 22, 2006.

2   *Gay Soul*, pages 52-53.

3   *Riddle*, pages 56-58.

4   *Riddle*, page 18.

5   *Gay Soul*, pages 110-111.

6   *Gay Soul*, page 115.

Practical Spirituality 11

Chapter

There's an old saying about being "so heavenly-minded that you're no earthly good" and that's certainly a good place to start in any consideration of being spiritual. It simply means that true spirituality demands that one be in touch with reality, that one's spirituality be grounded in reason as well as faith and mystical experience, in pragmatism, in what *is* rather than in what is wished. It means that it must be holistic in order to be holy, inclusive and mindful of all that we are, rather than prejudiced by favoring one aspect of self to the detriment of other aspects of self. That said, it probably means moderation, temperance, and a balanced and centered approach to believing, perceiving, and acting.

The dualism of many religions has sundered the body from the spirit, with the unintended result that spirituality is often relegated to a pew or prayer mat during a formal worship service. Indeed the most fervent believers often rue the lack of zeal by those who believe with less demonstration of their faith. Unfortunately too many dogmatists believe that dogma is the hallmark of true spirituality, that knowing and teaching "absolute" truth is what is necessary.

I think otherwise. Healthy spirituality, a realistic and productive faith life, is meant not to simply lead to doctrine and tenets of beliefs but rather to right living, that is, living in accordance with one's authentic self. Salvation is knowing one's true identity as a divine creature, in relationship with divinity, and empowered thusly to live a virtuous life. Salvation and lifestyle are never separate since lifestyle is always a reflection and expression of one's salvation.

The New Testament, for one example among many, is very clear:

> What does it profit, my brethren, if a man says he has faith but has not works? Can his faith save him? If a brother or sister is ill-clad and in lack of daily food, and one says to them, "Go in peace, be warmed and filled," without giving them the things needed for the body, what does it profit? So faith by itself, if it has no works, is dead. (James 2:14-17)

> For no good tree bears bad fruit, nor again does a bad tree bear good fruit; for each tree is known by its own fruit. For figs are not gathered from thorns, nor are grapes picked from a bramble bush. The good man out of the good treasure of his heart produces good, and the evil man out of his evil treasure produces evil; for out of the abundance of the heart his mouth speaks. (Luke 6:43-45)

> If I speak in the tongues of men and of angels, but I have not love, I am a noisy gong or a clanging cymbal. And if I have prophetic powers, and understand all mysteries and all knowledge and if I have faith, so as to remove mountains, but I have not love I am nothing. If I give away all I have, and if I deliver my body to be burned but have not love, I gain nothing.
> Love is patient and kind; love is not jealous or boastful; it is not arrogant or rude. Love does not insist on its own way; it is not irritable or resentful. It does not rejoice at wrong, but rejoices in the right. Love bears all things, believes all things, hopes all things, endures all things. (1 Corinthians 13:1-7)

It is for that reason that I wrote in the last chapter that

faith is meant to lead to the practice of virtue. If our faith (and the spirituality which encompasses it) has no practical application, if it does not direct and therefore have an effect on our actions, then it has no value. Yes, there may be some satisfaction in thinking that one is "saved," some pleasure in enjoying one's self-righteousness, but I suspect that such a spirituality is akin to the whitened sepulchers that Jesus used in his metaphors against the hypocrites of his age.

In the early eighties I was a married man struggling with a confused sexual identity. Though my wife and I were ostensibly in therapy to save our marriage, in private counseling I admitted that I could not resist having Gay sex. As much as I protested that I wanted to be heterosexual, I frequented adult bookstores, Gay bars, and bathhouses to satisfy my lust for sex with men. Finally one night my therapist told me his rule: "When a client says one thing and does another, I always listen to what they do."

Actions, you see, always speak louder than words. No amount of recitation of dogma, of repetition of doctrine, or of quoting of a sacred text says as much about one's spirituality as do one's actions.

Recognition of the connection between our beliefs and our actions is critical in attaining a balanced and happy life. Every action that we perform is a reflection of our faith. Here I do not simply mean that our lives merely reflect some philosophical or theological position. I mean that our actions are rooted and grounded in and emanate from what and how we believe. Faith is central to our actions. Even when we profess to believe in a certain way, our actions will reflect our actual beliefs, reflecting not only our faith but our doubt and confusion as well.

The paradigms that we believe determine our interpretation of reality. It is the credence or doubt we give to a perception along with our conscious and subconscious beliefs both positive (I know this will work.) and negative (Should I really be doing this?) that determine our actions and hence their outcomes.

Beyond just our paradigms, of course, everything is in some way connected to everything else.

Many people, of course, deny these connections. They allow their materialistic and scientific world view to be the only world view possible. They think that something done in secret, for instance, has no public effect, that something that happens at work won't reach into their bedroom, that events they consider separate are indeed separate. But the truth is that everything is connected. Knowing this truth we have an effective way to understand reality and hence direct our lives.

Spirituality and BDSM

As you read the following pages, keep in mind that BDSM is primarily what we do. As action it reflects our paradigms, our culture, and our beliefs. A healthy and well-articulated spirituality provides a sound basis for developing a vibrant kinky lifestyle. Additionally it provides rich and valid affirmation for our kink. One of the as yet unstated purposes of this book is to begin the creation of rationale that defends SM on philosophical, spiritual, and perhaps even religious grounds. Imagine the impact, for instance, of resting our self-defenses on freedom of Religion.

We need not go to such extremes. The assumptions and explanations in this book are perfectly valid if they do no more than to affirm and encourage each of us to accept the validity of our lifestyle and to pursue a practical life based on virtue and pleasure.

Let me continue then with a consideration of how one's spirituality ought to be practiced.

At this point I should probably remind you to "Do as I say, not as I do," but I won't. Instead I will remind you that practical spirituality, though it certainly has some generally applicable principles that can benefit all of us, is first and foremost an expression of your authentic self.

This then puts a burden on you to know yourself, which is a life-long task, a peeling away of self-deception and a process of learning through life-long experience and reflection on those experiences. Your path is uniquely your own and must be found not in a book or a lecture from some minister, teacher, or guru (authors included in this list) but within yourself. It requires self-appraisal and reflection. Without that basis your actions cannot be consistent with your real self, since that self will remain unknown to you.

Prayer

Long ago a friend noted that you can get the man out of the Catholic Church but that you probably can't get the Catholic Church out of the man. By prayer, without meaning to discount all of its other forms, I mean contemplation, which the nuns taught me was the highest form of prayer.

I wish that I could now speak to you in another language because as soon as I use the word "prayer" your old tapes, the paradigms of your own religious history or lack thereof, which are fundamental to your understanding of spiritual practice, are going to prejudice your understanding of what I just wrote. What I mean by prayer is time spent in communication, in observation, in communion, in listening, in simply resting in the presence of one's divine self and the Divine Self of which it is a part.

It is not asking. It is not seeking. It is not begging or even worshipping. It is not found in a book of prayer, in the recitation of litanies, psalms, or ejaculations (Yes we were taught to say ejaculations[1] in grammar school). Instead it is being with your self as yourself without distraction.

How you best do that is up to you to discover and then practice what you've learned. Over the years my "prayer life" has evolved as experiences have taught me an improved sense

175

of self. My practice now is an eclectic mixture of energy work and self-balancing, of sexual arousal and subspace floating, of theta reverie and a good nap. It is drifting and flying, sending my roots deep into the earth and my spirit high into the stars. It is all of that and none of that. It is particularly my time for myself, when the "myself" I meet is the god within me.

Prayer is first and foremost a time to pause the pendulum of my life in the center, to know that I am, for the moment, in balance. It is time to disregard all that is external so that I can experience the depth, height, breadth, and infinity of the Internal and Eternal. It is taking the time to breathe slowly and deeply, to listen quietly as an observer who neither edits nor comments, of experiencing the flow by going with it.

There is little of my prayer life that is formal. I pray in my dungeon. I pray in my classroom. I pray for seconds or for as long as I like. It is as simple as remembering to ground myself by feeling the earth or floor beneath me, or as "high church" as Gregorian chant, incense and candlelight.

A Life Worth Living

The practice of prayer in general and meditation in particular is not the goal of a spiritual life but rather the springboard to it. It is taking time to refuel, to reconnect, to restore one's soul to its rightful place within the complex organism we call ourselves.

Perhaps now you can see why I bothered with a chapter about paradigms and why I started with a consideration of brain waves and endorphins. They are all part, each in their unique way, of realizing a life worth living. How can we know ourselves if we don't take time to be in touch, in quiet communication, with ourselves and with all of the aspects of self that make us our very special and unique selves?

Without knowing the authentic self, which takes time and effort to achieve, we cannot choose that which is authentic for us.

Without listening to one's soul we can make only superficial decisions based on one impulse or another. Without quieting the various voices in "our head" we cannot bring their sounds into harmony. It is not that we silence any of them but that we let each take its proper place in the symphony of our life.

Virtue

Having done this, or begun to, we can then begin to know what is our virtuous path. The operative word here is "our." Right acting is not a dogmatic, "my way or the highway," sort of thing. Right acting is the result of being authentic within the circumstances in which one finds oneself.

There is, of course, a generally applicable meaning to the word virtue. It is the genuinely human way of acting and includes the four "Cardinal Virtues" of justice, prudence, fortitude, and temperance. My dictionary defines them thusly: Temperance is "moderation in action, thought, or feeling: restraint; habitual moderation in the indulgence of the appetites or passions: self-control." Prudence is "the ability to govern and discipline oneself by the use of reason; sagacity or shrewdness in the management of affairs: discretion; providence in the use of resources: economy; caution or circumspection as to danger or risk." Fortitude is "strength of mind that enables a person to encounter danger or bear pain or adversity with courage." Justice is "the maintenance or administration of what is just [having a basis in or conforming to fact or reason] especially by the impartial adjustment of conflicting claims or the assignment of merited rewards or punishments."

Subordinate to these are the virtues of gratitude, liberality, affability, sobriety, chastity, continence, humility, meekness, decorum, patience, munificence, magnanimity, and perseverance. I'll let you pull out your own dictionary to learn the meaning of these various ways of acting.

That said, it is the application of virtue to an individual's specific course of action that is important. Justice, for an example, is only a theoretical concept until we are faced with how we will act justly towards a neighbor. Practical spirituality, then, while it must be informed as to theory and ideas of right acting, must be more than theoretical. It must be active.

Mere lip service leads to hypocrisy. "What action flows from what you believe?" is the relevant question.

Creativity

Practical spirituality is open to the spirit, that is, it is willing to be inspired, to think "outside of the box," to open the heart and mind to new and perhaps alternate ways of thinking and therefore being and acting.

As I have explored consciousness over the years, one of the study's more significant effects has been to increase my creativity. Some of the credit for this goes to Conrad, since he strongly encouraged me to become more creative while I was a student at his New Age center. The center offered regular art lessons which even at $20.00 each I couldn't afford, so I did some thinking about how I could express my creativity at a lower cost. It was then that I began my first foray into writing -- and sold my first articles.

When I moved to Chicago a few years later, I had already had the experience of "professional writing" and was emboldened to suggest that I could write a column for Gay Chicago Magazine, a suggestion that eventually led to yours truly being as widely published as I am. Certainly I would not have thought that fourteen years' worth of weekly columns and six books would have come out of my being part of that Ft. Wayne center.

Creativity, though, is more than just art in its various forms. It is an integral part of problem solving, planning, and growth. Defined as "Ability to create," we can then find that to create means "To bring into existence; to invest with a new

178 form; to bring about by a course of action; to produce through

imaginative skill." Once again we see that there are two aspects to our topic, the first being thought, the second being action. Indeed the dictionary puts a great deal more emphasis on the doing than the thinking in this regard.

It reminds me of my stock answer to those who tell me they want to become writers. "What have you written?" I ask. When I get the usual answer of "Nothing," I remind them that one needs only to write to become a writer. Being a published writer, of course, entails more, but there's no chance of that happening until the aspiring writer actually writes. You can think about writing all you want; it is the practice of doing so that earns you the title. So it is with creativity in general. Having said that, though, I'll talk more about the thinking part than the doing part.

The practical side of one's spirituality determines one's openness to inspiration, to hear from the Muses if you like, or simply to be able to think of new ideas, new paths, and new actions. My spirituality, since it recognizes the presence of divinity within me, offers a paradigm wherein I can tap into the whole of the Universe in order to create.

Because I believe that I can be inspired, I am open to being inspired, whatever the source of that inspiration may be. There is no need here to get all "New Age woo-woo." Inspiration, I have found, comes from a myriad of sources, if we are but open to it. So on a given day I may write my column (to use a weekly example) based on inspiration found in a question emailed to me, or from something that happened at home or at school, or from something I read, experienced during my ride to college on the "L," or maybe thought of in the shower, in the dungeon, or when I woke up at 3 am to relieve my sixty year-old bladder. My point is that the sources of creativity are all around us.

The challenge is to notice them and hold on to them long enough that we can do something about them.

There is no mystique about this methodology. There are pads and pens scattered all around our home. I use them in

179

the dungeon (where I meditate and/or nap), in the bedroom (for those middle-of-the-night flashes), and in my knapsack (so I can jot something down during my commute). The availability of a way to remember the hints that come from the universe is a clear statement to my soul that when he (or is it a she or an it?) has something to say, I will listen.

I have learned this lesson the hard way. Too often I have gotten an idea and then lost it, thought of a great topic and failed to make note of it, or had a pithy sentence to add to my current manuscript, only to have it gone the next day when I was ready (and probably needed) to use it. Inspiration is only a hint, a breath, a quiet breeze and is too often soon long-gone if we don't do something to keep it.

Intuition

My mom used to joke that she was psychic. I think she was, though I suspect that to her it was more of a joke than a reality. Many of us think of psychic readers, astrologers, and those who use Tarot cards as phonies and charlatans. I'm not about to comment on the veracity of one or another "fortune teller," but I will comment on the phenomenon in general, since it is so closely related to creativity, as well as sexuality and spirituality.

Obviously, if you've read the last few paragraphs you know that I believe that inspiration is available to each of us. In fact I would say that the only problem I have with Extra Sensory Perception (ESP) is the word "extra." I have come to the conclusion that anyone who thinks that there are only five senses is missing the boat when it comes to their ability to sense. Everyone has the potential of using their psychic abilities, if they are just able to shift their paradigm to accept that fact. Once again, the materialism and scientism of our western culture often programs the awareness of such abilities out of our consciousness.

We relegate entities like angels, spirit friends, and inner

guides into the category of things for children and fools. We have the conceited and self-exalting idea that "other-world" phenomena are just that and don't belong in our world. Instead we believe that they belong to primitive and ancient societies, which is to say that many people think that such ideas are just part and parcel of an ignorant society.

I am reminded of a short sequence from "Voyager," where Seven of Nine and Chakotay are searching for two lost crew members. Seven notes that the tricorder in her hand indicates no life in the vicinity, when Chakotay says "They went this way." When questioned how he could possibly know that, he points to footprints in the planet's dust, noting that "You probably never had anyone teach you Native American tracking techniques."

Though we can all activate our intuition to some degree, it remains that we may have to un-learn some things in order to do so. As a teenager, for instance, I had a desire to explore occult and psychic phenomena. Unfortunately my Roman Catholic upbringing had taught me that to do so was a "mortal sin," so I avoided Tarot cards, psychic readers, and séances like a plague that would send me directly to Hell. It was only when I was freed from the constraints of another's morality that was I able to discover the power available from within my own being, that my soul would speak to me, if I would only listen.

The openness which I am encouraging is not simply waiting for some angelic appearance. It is being open to the world in which we live. As I said above, we can be inspired by a universe of sources and the mundane ones are just as important, if not as flashy, as the "spiritual" ones.

How then do we activate our intuition? The short answer is that we develop a greater sensitivity to sensing. We are all sensitive. The operative word here is greater and that takes practice. Just as we all have muscles that can lift, only exercise can develop them to the point where we can lift greater weights.

I would never have thought that developing my own ESP was possible until I was presented with the idea in Ft. Wayne. Specifically we were offered a class in remote viewing, that is seeing objects telepathically.[2] In three weeks we learned enough to test what we had learned. As it turned out I was going to be in Myrtle Beach, NC when the "final exam" was given. No problem. Instead of viewing from about six or seven blocks away, I could do so across the hundreds of miles that separated Steve Lewis (the sender) and me (the receiver). At the agreed upon time he viewed an object and I went into a quiet and darkened bedroom, relaxed, and "sensed." We did the exercise twice, once on each of two consecutive days.

The first day I sensed something black and round, warm and comfortable. I figured I had really flunked this test as I had no idea upon what Steve was focusing. Later that day we talked about it on the phone. I described what I "saw" and he congratulated me, as he had been looking at hot black coffee in a black cup.

The next day's sighting was just as enigmatic. There appeared in my thoughts running water and a large silver circle, like a tennis racket. Later I asked Steve if he had been taking a walk in the park, which was located on the banks of the St. Joseph River and where there were tennis courts. My guess was about six blocks off. Instead he had gone to a pocket park near where he worked (I knew it well) and had looked at a large, racket-shaped lamp with a huge silver globe that was in the middle of a fountain. I had seen it remotely, with the help of his eyes.

What, then, are some of the qualities necessary to develop an ability such as this? First of all, I think that we need to intend to become more aware of the intuitive information that floods us daily. It is not that we aren't already intuitive, but rather that we simply ignore our intuition. Intending to act otherwise means that we take time to listen, which requires a patient and diligent outlook. It's not, after all, as if we can just turn these abilities on and off, any more than we can simply decide to be a weight lifter or marathon runner and it is so. We have to devote time to study and to practice. Most importantly we have to quiet the noise of everyday living. If we are continually flooding our minds with trash TV, frenzied activity, and frivolity, we won't ever hear that still quiet voice deep beneath the din.

This is where the roles of relaxation and meditation come into play. They are the basic exercises that strengthen the connection to our inner self, thereby connecting us more fully to the universe in which that self lives.

By now my slave Patrick is asking "What does all this have to do with sex and SM?" A great deal, I would answer. Great sex, whether kinky or vanilla, demands a strong connection with one's partner. There is a great deal of intuition, of mind-reading, of being on the "same track" between partners who achieve the highest states of sexual pleasure. Without the attunement of one's intuition to another's thoughts, you may have a good time, but believe me when I say that it won't be as good as it gets.

Self-Esteem

Integral to accepting one's abilities, be they "extra" or mundane, is the place of one's self conception. What we think about who we are is probably the most important thought we can have. If we stifle ourselves with the idea that we are unworthy, incapable, failing, faulty, or somehow less-than, we will live that kind of life. Once again we come up on the necessity of knowing the authentic self.

Spirit is the interface between the soul and the body. It's the transformer, the stepping-down device that allows the soul to penetrate and enliven the physical body. I used to think about this theoretically, but last spring I experienced what I believe was my soul. I was in a workshop doing extensive breath work when I found myself in an altered state of consciousness. I was lying on the floor in a luminous field of golden light. I was utterly clear that it was my soul and that it was interpenetrating my body. I had always imagined that my soul was very tiny and that it lived in my heart. Much to my surprise, it was much bigger than my body, and my body was floating in it, like a fish floating in the sea.

In healthy, organic cultures, somehow the soul is able to weave itself into the body completely, harmoniously. But in this culture, where we distrust our bodies and deny that people have some kind of energy that is both indwelling and yet greater than the body, the soul has a lot of trouble getting in.[3]

I wish I could sell bottles of High Esteem Tonic, the drinking of which would automatically show the consumer his or her real worth, but I can't. You must explore your own self-image, shifting and sorting the myriad images you find there, deciding what should be kept and nurtured and what should be sent to the rubbish heap of deceiving, unreal poppycock.

It is your sole responsibility to know what is authentic about who you are, to cultivate yourself, to love yourself, and to rid yourself of the years' worth of impediments to doing so that have been heaped upon you by family, friends, and society. You are not, after all, the put-down, fragile, unloved kid who didn't make the baseball team. You are not incapable and unlovable. You are uniquely wonderful, talented, and holy, and you need only rid yourself of the negativity thrust upon you by those who wanted you to conform to their projections of who you are and how they thought you should live.

Since I can't market that tonic, I will remind you that when I write "you need only rid yourself" I am writing a mouthful. It is a life-long process but one well worth the effort.

Perception

It is, after all, a matter of perception. Who do you see when you look in the mirror? Can you see that image eye-to-eye and honestly say "I love what I see"? Though Harry Hay, a Gay activist from the latter half of the twentieth century, uses terms that may not hit home precisely in your situation, they speak clearly of seeing ourselves as we ought, freed from the constraints imposed by others:

> Humility is what is required here, not the arrogance of the hetero male who says there is either his way of seeing or none at all. That's a Eurocentric way of seeing. There are all kinds of windows on the world. We are so accustomed to thinking that our hetero, male, white world is the only world that is. The nonlinear mindsets coming to us from Africa, Indonesia, and Asia have many ways of perceiving. And until we are open to them all we're not going to be able to hear the actual marvelous world of stars and wind that is coming to us from all kinds of different places.[4]

Reflecting on Philosophy In the Dungeon

Experienced players are quick to note that intuition is an important guide in their ability to top during a scene. Though there is certainly a reliance on good negotiation and body language, they still understand the necessity of being centered in themselves and sensitive to the action of the play and the responses of their partners.

This book in general and this chapter in particular leave out more than they say. I hope you realize that right acting is based on a real desire to do well; that prayer comes in many forms, and that what is written here is just as much a reflection of my personal history as it is of anything else.

The challenge is to live as you believe you should everywhere, which is to say consistently. That means that you need to find ways to express your faith sexually as well as religiously. It is your mission to decide what such a sexuality means to you and to live that decision faithfully.

---

1   In this case an ejaculation is a short prayer, such as "Jesus have mercy." We were encouraged to repeat ejaculations often.

2   As a textbook we used *The Alexandria Project*, by Stephan A. Schwartz, Backinprint.com, 2001.

3   *Gay Soul*, pages 75-76.

4   *Gay Soul*, page 91.

Sex Magic 12

The he problem we are going to face in reading this chapter is the same challenge I addressed in the last. Just as the word "prayer" is loaded with all sorts of meanings and feelings, so too is the word "magic," and perhaps even more so. Prayer, at least, is sanctioned by the powers that form the status quo, while for the most part, magic is not.

Now you can probably guess from the last paragraph that I am neither talking about slights of hand or parlor tricks nor about evil or deceptive practices but of what my dictionary calls "The use of means (as charms, spells) believed to have supernatural power over natural forces." Alas, even my dictionary doesn't get it right.

The processes which we call "magical" are simply ones for which we cannot derive "natural" causation, since in our scientific, philosophical, and theological conceit anything that doesn't fit into our (ill-defined) paradigms must needs be sloughed off into the trash bin of the weird and un-natural. Far be it from me (he wrote tongue-in-cheek) to redefine the word magic, but I will. Magic is "the application of little-known, undiscovered, or un-believed laws of nature to produce results that are naturally consistent with those laws."

Having said that, let's go back to the dictionary. Note that the definition we read therein has two points to ponder. The first one is found in the word "believed" and the second in the word "supernatural."

I hope that I have shown that believing is an integral part of human existence. After all, would you go to bed if you didn't believe that you would be alive in the morning? Would you enjoy a sunset if you didn't believe there would be a sunrise? In any case, you might want to reread the chapter on "According to Your Faith." The dictionary version of magic is very consistent with what I have thus far written, as long as you note that there is the necessity of belief in the application of the means that are used.

Just as believing that the sun will come up, that aspirin is good for headaches, and that a car will take us down the highway, so too will those magical "means" (to be discussed later in this chapter) have some power, if we believe that they will effect a result.

My second observation has to do with the word "supernatural." Unfortunately we too often have the idea that supernatural somehow implies out of the natural, apart from the natural, and, of course, un-natural, which is to say against the natural. In truth the word supernatural simply alludes to the fact that there are some things, in the natural order of things, that are "super," that is they are above others. Supernatural only points to a hierarchy in what is natural.

Unfortunately we are way too limited in our understanding of nature and therefore follow that dog-gone tendency to see everything in terms of duality. We believe that supernatural must be the opposite of natural, rather than seeing that there is a total unity between that which is above and that which is below. Supernatural simply refers to that part of nature which is above the part that we know and understand.

You know, I hope, that we don't know everything, nor do we understand everything either. Let's not let our intellectual conceit get in the way of reality.

Now just in case you think that I arrived at this restatement of magic all by myself, look at what Albert Pike said of magic in his book, *Morals and Dogma*, published in 1871: "The Secret of the Occult Sciences is that of Nature itself, the Secret of the generation of the

Angels and Worlds, that of the Omnipotence of God.[1]

You see, when we know and understand all the laws of nature as they apply at all levels of nature and hence include the supernatural, then we will no longer have anything to call magical, which if you think about it, may not really be a very happy turn of events. So there is no secret word, no ancient talisman, or obscure ritual that's going to turn your pound of lead into gold, make elephants fly, or cure the common cold in contradiction to the laws of nature. On the other hand, there is the possibility that some day we will have learned enough about how nature works to do any and all of those things.

Think about each of them. Physics has taught us that both lead and gold are composed of protons, neutrons, and electrons, so there is the possibility of altering the number and configuration of those subatomic particles in order to change one element into the other. Elephants can fly, if you get them into an airplane. How magical is a jet-liner or even the Wright Brothers' biplane for that matter? Before they were invented I am sure there were a lot of people who believed that flying, let alone walking on the moon, would be a "supernatural" act. As for the common cold, well let's give the doctors a few more years. Many childhood diseases that were fatal a hundred or so years ago are nearly gone -- if you but get your vaccines. Was Dr. Salk a magician? No, but he understood the laws of biology well enough to develop the means to eradicate polio.

We need only to take the information presented thus far in order to understand and use magic, a term I will use because it sounds a lot sexier than "natural processes derived from as yet hidden laws of nature."

If you remember that married couple building a house in chapter ten, "According to Your Faith," then you will recall the application of magic. It works this way. Conceive of that which you want to manifest, apply the necessary energy to its manifestation, and await the result.

Now for most things this process is pretty easy. I want breakfast, I do what it takes to get it, and the end result is probably ready in less than half an hour. More difficult manifestations require more time, more faith, or more energy and hence seem more magical than others. In fact what we call magic (as if all of life isn't magical enough) is that process in which we formalize and structure our desires in order to clarify them, increase our energy, and perform rituals to hasten the result so that we need less rather than more patience, to get that which we want. For those reasons we use the term "Magic."

Bonewits' Definition

In his book *Real Magic*, Isaac Bonewits defines magic as

> Magic: (I) A general term for arts, sciences, philosophies and technologies concerned with (a) understanding and using various altered states of consciousness within which it is possible to have access to and control over one's psychic talents, and (b) the uses and abuses of those psychic talents to change interior and/or exterior realities. (2) A science and an art comprising a system of concepts and methods for the build-up of human emotions, altering the electrochemical balance of the metabolism, using associational techniques and devices to concentrate and focus this emotional energy, thus modulating the energies broadcast by the human body, usually to affect other energy patterns whether animate or inanimate, but occasionally to affect the personal energy pattern. (3) A collection of rule-of-thumb techniques designed to get one's psychic talents to do more or less what one wants, more often than not, one hopes. It should be obvious that these are thaumaturgical definitions [i.e., having to do with the miraculous].[2]

190

Bonewits' definition leads us to the further consideration of many of the points we have thus far covered. In order to clarify our conception and increase our energy, we enter an altered state. There are various rituals (techniques) for doing this. Once we are in an altered state we are in better control of our own talents and abilities which naturally reside within us as partakers of the divine life.

The easiest way to discuss these techniques is to look at them in terms of their steps or parts, such as thought, action, and tools. I would list them as follows:

- Intent
- Form
- Altered State
- Visualization or Declaration
- Transformation
- Close

Intent

As "In the beginning was the Word," so too magical manifestation begins with an idea. As Napoleon Hill wrote, "What the mind can conceive, man can achieve."[3] This is not, unfortunately, an easy proposition. Too often our thinking lacks clarity, hence Bonewits' note that magic only does "more or less what one wants, more often than not, one hopes." Written differently, one hopes that magic more or less works (meaning we get what we want). Getting exactly what we want often requires a clarity of thought and faith that too often we can only approximate, not attain. Our thought processes are limited. We do not know everything, can not plan for every eventuality, and seldom understand exactly what we are doing or getting. To this very human lack of precision is added the fact that we probably don't have as great and powerful a faith as we might need.

Hence, though we can intellectually assent to the idea that "Anything is possible," we must also understand that not everything is probable. The "more or less" is determined by how much or how little we know and by the extent of our believing and doubting. It is for this reason that we turn to form, that is the

> established method of expression or proceeding: procedure according to rule or rote; manner or style of performing or accomplishing according to recognized standards of technique; the structural element, plan, or design of a work or art.

Now I have a confession to make. As a somewhat Red-Painted Face practitioner (i.e., eclectic and non-traditional), I'm not a very good source for an essay on the form of magic ritual. I tend to be very "low church," though I will admit that I find satisfaction and effectiveness in what I do and I am probably more ritualistic than I admit. Some of this, of course, boils down to advice I was given just after I graduated from college: "KISS. Keep it simple, stupid."

There are three other reasons for my tendency to keep my ritual simple. The first is just a case of laziness. The second is that I believe that faith and intent contribute more to manifestation than do procedure. And thirdly, as one who has spent a lot of time in mainline churches (at least I used to) I have found that it is far too easy for ritual to become rote and therefore ineffectual.

I don't have a lot of time for long and complex statements. I prefer the simple and the direct. You'll never find me writing a definition of magic as complete as Bonewits', though I am perfectly content to believe it and to quote it.

Still, the Catholic boy in me understands that there is a serious and necessary place for ritual in our lives. We are physical beings and the physical aspects of form speak to that part of us. Ritual is an effective way to focus our minds and hearts and as such it may not only be extremely helpful but is probably necessary as well.

The caveat I add to this thinking is that we need to take care that ritual doesn't lose its meaning and its efficacy, that our ritual must reflect that which is authentic to us. For this reason, you'll not find that "one size fits all" nor that you will practice one form of ritual "'til death do you part." Ritual is, after all, just as changing as the rest of our lives and needs to grow as we grow.

Changing Our Focus

Ritual, then, is the form and practice one uses to change one's focus and to aid the mind/body thought/power connection in manifesting that which is desired. To elaborate, changing our focus entails words and actions that help us to hone in more closely on what exactly it is we intend to have, do, or receive, and to clarify our thoughts and feelings, centering them more intensely on our objectives while they remove distractions, and "get us in the mood."

To create a comfortable space, one that is a conducive atmosphere for performing magic, is the first goal of ritual. This process, for me, means things like raising or lowering the temperature in my dungeon or bedroom to a comfortable level, dimming the lights, lighting candles, and selecting appropriate music. Each of these activities helps me to clear away distractions. With less distraction I can obviously better focus my thoughts and intentions.

The form of ritual also creates what we call a "Sacred Space" within which we feel protected and are better able to raise our level of energy so that we attain the Altered State of

Consciousness necessary to create in this way.

Sacred Spaces

Here we run into one of those usual contradictions. When we ask "What is sacred?" we find it means "made holy; set apart to religious use; consecrated; not profane or common; as, a sacred place; a sacred day; sacred service," thereby returning to yet another conception of duality. The problem I have, of course, is that this definition is not holistic. It sets the sacred apart from the mundane. In my book everything is sacred. How can we label something less than sacred when all is One?

On the other hand, I recognize that there is specialness in creating that which our physical senses would call a sacred space. We are limited in our ability to focus and to direct our attention solely (or mostly) in one direction. Therefore in realization and acceptance of our pervasive attention deficit, putting ourselves in a space that is set apart is probably a good idea.

An altered state is, after all, just that. It is different than the state we were in when we began and in order to alter our inner state we most often have to alter our external state as well. Ritual recognizes this need and facilitates the shift. As I mentioned above, the elements of ritual include such physical factors as lighting, temperature, sound, feel, quiet, and privacy, all of which add to our sense of both safety and sacredness. Additionally such elements can be tremendous aids in the arousal of memory, thereby altering both our inner space and our energy.

Form

The structure of the ritual itself, including actions and words, can be as diverse as the uniqueness of the individual utilizing the structure. Often this structure is determined by the leaders of the group or by the group itself, so that the form is one that resonates with its participants.

The circle has long been part of mysticism, occultism, and religion, especially in Pagan or Wiccan environments. It is especially honored in groups where sharing and consensus are more important than in ones where oligarchic or highly defined leadership is the norm. Placing ourselves in a circle allows for freer sharing and a greater ease of mutual communication. It promotes the "each to every" rather than the "one to many" modality.

As Philip and Stephanie Carr-Gomm write in *The Druid Animal Oracle*:

> When we let go of believing we are superior, we open ourselves to the experience of living in the community of Nature -- being a part of it, not separate from it. We are welcomed back into the circle we really never left, except in our delusion. The Round Table is made complete again. In Druidry, we come together in circles -- seated in a circle around the fire, in a circle of stones or a grove of trees. And as we do this, we come to experience that we are in communion not just with our present-day physical companions, but with the spirits of the animals and trees, the stones and the stars, with our ancestors and our children and the children who will come when we have long passed into the Summerlands. Looking up into the night sky, we sense the animal spirits looking down on us -- and we understand why the ancient Greeks named the circle of the constellations the zodiac -- which means "the circle of living animals." [4]

The circle represents a very important paradigm, that of equality. Whereas many traditional structures are one to many, emphasizing the primacy of this or that preacher or priest, the circle, as shown in the illustration, emphasizes an important each to every relationship.

195

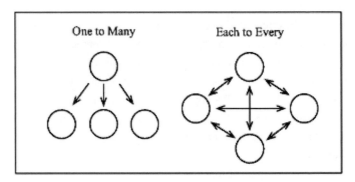

Illustration Five [5]

The circle is a symbol -- universal, unending, everywhere equal -- of our coming together as well as a communication device -- all encompassing, non-hierarchical, all-inclusive. By its nature it encompasses all directions, and our rituals often reflect that reality, recognizing in both action and in word the East, South, West, North, Up, Down, and therefore the infinite number of directions included in those directions, such as Southeast and "Up and to the Right."

To the directions we then add the Elements, in this case, Air, Fire, Water, and Earth. These tend to be nearly universal symbols for all of creation and are found mentioned in various cultures. That's not to say that there aren't variations, nor that you cannot use other elements that you find more appropriate.

What I am describing here comes out of my own experience, my study, and what I have been shown by people who have shared their knowledge and experience with me. In the final analysis, as you will see later, I have picked and chosen eclectically so that the circle I create is most comfortable for me. Nevertheless there is a lot to be said by recognizing historical connections and other traditions, as doing so gives us a sense of the unity with all tribes and cultures that have gone before us and are present around us, and adds immeasurably to our own knowledge and understanding.

It's important to recall, as I noted in the Introduction, that my experiences are limited. This chapter therefore reflects both my knowledge and my ignorance. There are many paths and many traditions, each of which presents us with the possibility of finding some wisdom. I therefore urge you to find, experiment with, and discover the rituals and elements of magic that are most authentic to you.

So I use incense to symbolize the Air, as the smoke of the incense makes the Air visible and the smell permeates the circle as does the air itself. I light a special candle, brighter than the others I use, to represent Fire, though I add to Fire the idea of Desire, bringing to mind the fire of passion and the heat of desire. Water is what it is, though once again it is a reminder of life itself. We are born out of the water of the womb. A human body is composed mostly of water. We need water on a daily basis to live. The Bible talks about the water of life and many traditions use water for purification. Water also reminds us of thirst and this is a great time to seek the quenching of thirst as in our thirst for wisdom. Lastly Earth is that which sustains us. In this case I use salt, as in salt of the earth. It is a symbol of strength and nurturing as earth provides us a sure place to stand and bountiful produce to feed our bodies.

To each of these elements is connected a totem animal. Here you will find the widest variety in the elements of a circle, as totem animals tend to be more personally recognized. For instance, I was never quite comfortable with the Bear that I was told belonged in the north. Often I would call that animal a Bull, until I just admitted that for me, the animal of strength and power was indeed a Bull. Later, when I began to find a greater affinity with Dionysos, the Bull made more sense, as that is one of his representative animals.

197

In the east I put the eagle, the animal that flies on the air. An eagle's keen sight represents, for me, the all-seeing eye of knowledge. In the south I find the lion, Lord of the desert and hence of heat, roaring with passion, dominant and powerful, the King of the Beasts. In the west I recognize the sea snake or serpent, swimming and ruling the waters, a symbol of Neptune, a mighty water dragon.

Others have other methodologies and explanations. Here is what Ed Steinbrecher had to say in *Gay Soul*:

> Tarot cards also have four suits, which represent the four bodies that each of us have. They correspond to fire, earth, air, and water. The physical body has to do with the earth quality. The emotional, or astral body, is water. The air body contains all our thinking -- the three modes of thought: logic, comparison, and gestalt. And the last body, the one that vibrates the highest, is the fire body, which contains our abilities to give love, create, and be alive.[6]

The Basic Methodology

What I do, then, is to create a circle. I usually do so in my dungeon or bedroom, though any appropriate gathering place may certainly be used. When the same space is used repeatedly it begins to take on the characteristics of the circle, holding for us memories of past gatherings, and becoming ever more comfortable. I had a small dungeon in my home in Ft. Wayne, Indiana and I found that after months and years of use as my place to create my sacred space, it remained that way all the time, as if the energies I invoked and created there remained.

Before I create a circle, I know why I am doing so. Remember that in all of this the place of intention is important. Realistically most of my circles are created for very general reasons, such as balancing my own energy, becoming more attuned to the universe, or simply listening to my soul. On occasion I will create a circle to listen to the Universe and await inspiration. (Remember that most often it is about having fun.)

Two summers ago, as an example, I was struggling to write my last book and, having had a stressful first half of the year, felt very burnt out. The manuscript was going nowhere and I was at a point of physical and emotional exhaustion, partly because of the stress of having bought and moved into a house that needed work and partly because my brother and I had to deal with serious illnesses with both of our parents. By August, when the summer session at school was over, I found myself simply retreating nearly every afternoon to my dungeon where I would create a simple circle, one with little more than four votive lights and lots of intentions to sleep in the comfort of a safe environment. The intention was to renew myself and wait for inspiration. In four week's time both came to me in torrents.

First I will prepare the space, turning on the heater, if necessary, and the music, lowering the lights and lighting a small votive candle in each of the primary directions (East, South, West, and North). I begin in the East as that is how I was taught. Only later did I learn that this has something to do with the rising Sun. I also place a symbol of the elements next to each candle.

When I am ready, I will disrobe, since I almost always do my magic in the nude, or as more discreet Pagans say "Sky clad." As you may have guessed, most of my magic is explicitly sexual in nature. I can't, after all, think of a better way to raise my energy level and to alter my consciousness than by becoming sexually aroused. This book is, after all, about Philosophy In the Dungeon. You wouldn't want me to disappoint you, would you?

I would like to remind you that there is a very simple danger in the following paragraphs. Writing down my practices may lead some readers to think they are special formulas. They are not. I write them here only to give an example upon which

199

you can experiment and find your own voice, your own formula. Just as there can be power in the Alleluia chorus sung with vigor, devotion, and the right direction, so can the same words become dull repetition and empty rote. I caution you therefore not to read the following as anything more than suggestions that work for me, and fodder for your own creative process.

Though I am using invocations that are in the plural, many of my circles are done in solitude, i.e., I am alone. That said, I am never alone but rather am the only human present. In that sense the "we" and the "us" refers to me and my guarding angels, friendly entities, and totem animals.

Now I am ready to invoke the circle.

I go to the East, raise my arms and say:

> Hail Eagle, God of the East, Lord of the Earth. We call you. Come here and join us. Create this circle with us. Fly to us, Eagle, bring us sight, knowledge, and wisdom. Teach us to see. Help us create this circle. Protect and guide us.

Now I will light the incense.

> Eagle, we greet you. Thank you for your presence.

Then I will walk to the South and likewise raise my arms and say:

> Hail Lion, God of the South, Lord of Fire, Lord of Desire. We call you. Come here and join us. Create this circle with us. Join with Eagle to create this circle, bring us passion, light, and love and desire. Warm our hearts in fellowship. Raise our energy and give us power. Teach us to love as we ought. Create the circle with us to protect and guide us.

200

Here I will light the candle.

Lion, we greet you. Thank you for your presence.

Moving to the West, I do the same, saying:

Hail Serpent, Water Dragon, Behemoth, God of the West, Lord of the Water, of the Seas, the Oceans, the Rivers, Lakes, and Streams, the Dew, the Clouds, and the Rains. We call you. Come here and join us. Create this circle with us. Join Eagle and Lion, bring us your holy water, quench our thirst, give us life. Teach us to live and to flow, to nourish all as you nourish us. Create the circle to protect and guide us.

Here I will sprinkle some water.

Serpent, we greet you. Thank you for your presence.

Lastly I move to the North and say:

Hail Bull, God of the North, Lord of Earth, Powerful and strong God, Salt of the Earth. We call you. Come here and join us. Create this circle with us. Join Eagle, Lion, and Serpent to create this circle, make us strong. Give us your strength while you nourish us to live and work. Lend your power to us. Raise our energy and give us strength. Teach us to be as strong as we need. Create the circle to protect and guide us. Make the circle complete.

Here I will pick up a pinch of salt and scatter it..

Bull, we greet you. Thank you for your

presence.

Having thus created my circle I will return to its center, invoking the Sky God, using the names of Zeus, Heavenly Father, Shiva, and Dionysos, and the Earth Goddess, the Mother. I especially recognize my place as a human between Sky Father and Earth Mother. I am the bridge, the link, between the two, uniquely their child, the point where spirit and matter are divinely joined in a special, holy way.

Now anything goes. I might spend some time meditating or doing some visualizations that balance my energy, connecting all the directions. I might just rest in the peace or begin to have sex.

Raise Energy Level

Within the psychic safety of a circle, I will then raise my energy level through meditation, visualization, sexual activity, or as is more usual a combination of these activities. The use of sexual activity to alter my consciousness, that is, raise my energy level, depends upon whether I am alone or in a circle with a partner or partners, not that I'm opposed to self arousal when I'm alone.

When the activity is more about meditation or balancing, I allow the flow of thoughts to guide my time in the circle. My "thinking" becomes more a matter of watching my thoughts and letting my mind wander. I will sometimes "actively" meditate or recite a mantra and at other times, just allow myself to drift, even to sleep.

If the ritual is going to have a sexual component, then I just begin a scene and play. It is as simple as that. I trust that the universe enjoys what we do and that doing so will alter my consciousness so that I will be better able to focus my mind on my intention, if indeed I need to do that. As I noted above, not all our magic needs to be dedicated to a specific goal. Over the years, most of my intentions have focused on more general character development, to use an appropriate term.

So for years I prayed (yes that is a valid form of magic) to receive more of the Holy Spirit and sometimes, of course, I still do. I have used ritual to seek wisdom, balance, and right relationships. I have used magic, over the course of time, to open myself to inspiration, as when I did magic to aid in writing my last book and this one as well. The basic challenge in all of this is to be in touch with one's authentic self, open to what the universe will send us, as we remain balanced, grounded, centered, and ready to live a true and practical spirituality.

Sexual magic is my preferred methodology because it is most natural to my horny, randy, and lusty self. I have also found it effective, though that's not to say that another path might not be equally authentic and effective for you. For me, sexual activity liberates me into a close connection with the universe, reminds me of the basic unity I share with all, and aligns me with Reality, or as Joseph Kramer says:

> The question is: How do we get in alignment with ourselves? I feel orgasm--not ejaculation, but orgasm--is a major aligning process. It's a vibration that's so powerful that we get pulled in and we're fully present. It takes something extraordinary to bring the different facets of ourselves together. And for me that's prolonged, full-bodied orgasm.[7]

Having attained the power of the divine at the moment of orgasm, I then name, visualize, or in some way conceptualize that which I intend to manifest. In other words I envision the manifestation of what it is that I intend, believing and receiving the reality of that which I want to create.

Note, too, that a circle, especially one with several participants, can be done for several intentions, though by doing

203

so one risks diluting the energy among those intentions. For that reason I try to make sure that my intentions are generally related. On the other hand, the more participants the greater the possibility of there being a higher level of energy and therefore more power to share among various intentions.

Intention

It is important here to restate that a holistic approach is of the utmost importance. It's not simply a matter of wishing to win the lottery or of besting one's adversaries by performing some ritual and getting what you want. Magic is not a matter of knowing what buttons to push but rather of being in tune, in balance, with the Universe so that your intentions are aligned with the Will of the Divine.

We share in that will and are co-creators in that which will be. On the other hand, no one of us is a supreme despot with the solitary power of complete control. We are connected to all that is. I hope you understand that the connection is for the better, even if it thwarts what we think is for our best.

In simple terms and direct terms,

Be careful what you pray for.

Too often we have a blind spot to what we believe we want. Not every fantasy, to be sure, ought to be realized. The laws of nature will not be mocked. We reap that which we sow, the shadow side of our selves is just as operative as the light, and there are times, more often than we like, when we really don't know what's best for us.

Let me illustrate this with a true story.

In 1993 I was a computer salesman and was failing to attain my monthly sales quotas. I had been asked by my manager to try and sell our products to the City of Chicago and over the previous seven or eight months had failed miserably, though I had begun to learn how the system worked. Then my manager found a bid solicitation from the City for more than 600 computers and peripherals and I spent three weeks putting together the bid, including securing a hundred thousand dollar performance bond.

One evening, about a week before the bid was due, my friend and fuck-buddy Jerry came over for sex and we had a rousing good time. I had been using sex magic on occasion but hadn't as of yet shared my ideas with Jerry, nor with very many other people for that matter. As you'll see I hadn't yet "perfected the process" and I didn't open a sacred circle for protection. As they say, "Fools rush in."

My opportunity to sell those 600 computers was foremost in my mind that night, as was a lawsuit that Jerry had pending against the City for an act of police violence. Before we began having sex, we had talked and he told me that the case which had been pending for more than several years was finally about to get its day in court.

Jerry and I had a great night of sex, his masochism matching my sadistic desires and both of our libidos more than willing to arouse and satisfy each other. Eventually I mounted Jerry from behind, my hard cock rammed up his willing ass.

It's difficult to describe what happened next, as words can't convey the fullness of the experience. Simply put, I found myself in an altered state. The longer version of the story is that I felt Jerry transform into an eagle and I rode his back as we flew with the clouds into the high atmosphere. Whether or not we reached outer space I can't tell but it was an ecstatic flight.

In that state, an orgasm of great intensity overtook my body and I was in a place of light and power. Immanently, immediately, or right after (I don't know for certain, as there was no perception of time to this part of the event) I thought of those computers and mentally accepted that I had presented the winning bid. As an after-thought I thought that Jerry's lawsuit would be successful as well.

With that, we slowly settled onto the bed in peaceful silence, enjoying the afterglow.

The following Wednesday, the due date to submit the bid, I was ready. To my amazement there was only one other company in competition with me and they were disqualified for having failed to present the required bond. My bid was opened and I won. I walked back to the office in tears. I had won a bid to sell more than $700,000 of equipment. I was dazed and delighted and amazed at the power of sex magic.

That weekend I went on a vacation to Arizona with another friend, a trip that had been planned for months.

I returned excited at the prospects for my career, only to find that in spite of doing my best and having had a senior manager review my bid and check my math, the bid that I had submitted contained three critical errors, which totaled $200,000. What was a $700,000 bid should have been $900,000. The performance bond assured that my company would deliver the bid as specified and at the lower cost. It also assured that I lost my job that very same day.

Remember that I wrote "Be careful what you pray for." I got what I sought, but unfortunately I had failed to ask that the winning bid be correct and profitable. The irony is, of course, that under the circumstances of the bid's delivery, a price of $900,000 would have still won.

A week or so later, Jerry won his lawsuit.

Experienced magicians know that one's intention needs to be clear and that ill-conceived or evil intentions will come back to haunt them. Magic, either impressive or mundane, is always in tune with the Universe and its natural laws. It therefore behooves one seeking to manifest to do his or her homework and know what they are seeking and to seek it well.

At the root of my desire to win that bid was a deeper and more holistic desire to find success. I had failed, after all, at two previous jobs as a computer salesman and was failing at this one. Once unemployed I gave up the pursuit of that career, spending the summer looking for a teaching position and writing my first book.

This eventually led to a long term position as a part-time college instructor and a full-time writer, which of course brought me to the here and now, a successfully published author and national speaker. I can honestly and thankfully say that the ritual I did with Jerry changed my life for the better, even if at the time I didn't know what the future held and certainly didn't feel good about being fired. In fact, I won the bid to lose a job and lost a job to win a much better career.

A Caution Repeated

In my earliest studies of Tantra it seemed that every book I opened began with a chapter written by a stern and foreboding guru who insisted that what he was teaching in this volume was dangerous enough that it should only be attempted under the close supervision of an experienced teacher. Similar warnings are found in various books of Magic. Even modern day practitioners of Wicca are careful to establish their sacred circles with the intent of protection and safety.

The moral here is that a little bit of knowledge can be a dangerous thing. Just because I believe that the Universe is a friendly place doesn't mean that every action is caused by friendliness. Once again, then, I encourage you to prepare yourself well, listen to experts in these matters, and take a slow, easy approach.

Altered States

Ritual is about change. We do it in order to bring about that which we intend, something not yet in existence except in the world of thought. Change, though, isn't always as easy or pleasant as one might wish. Some change comes only with difficulty and trauma. Fields, after all, have to be plowed before they can be planted.

One of the things that we often fail to remember when we invoke change, is that it is we who will change as well. As Ed Steinbrecher said

> We can't change something unless we are willing to change ourselves. If we change, everything changes.
> Everything is connected to everything else. [8]

Altered states can mean something as simple as changing our feelings and attitudes or the way we perform an action to something as dramatic (or traumatic) as ecstatic bliss, heavenly visions, and out-of-body experiences. They can be induced in a myriad of ways, as nearly any experienced BDSM player will tell you.

In the subculture of alternate sex we use pain, pleasure, intimacy, and other forms of stimulation. Historically believers have used fasting, penance, long sessions of prayer, chanting, dancing, and meditation. Some cultures, such as Native American, use natural, hallucinatory herbs. In a not-so-acceptable way some people use drugs and alcohol. I'm going to let you choose your path to the states necessary to create magically. I will only caution that it be healthy and holistic.

Change, then, demands our openness, our willingness to change in order that there might be change. Therefore we need to understand the implications of change as well as the areas where change is necessitated.

Too often our thoughts fail to remember all that is involved in the change we wish to create. We think that there are areas which will have no influence on the changes that we seek, that they are somehow not a part of what we intend, that there is a separation that means that a change in this state won't affect another state. Hence we think that what we want will happen the way we want it, in ignorance of the greater unity of the universe.

But the Universe never fails to be itself, never violates its own laws, and we get the full result of that which we intend, not just the part that we wished for.

Perception and Sight

It's important then that we see clearly and act authentically as we move into these areas of higher creativity and manifestation. For most of us, and probably all of us, that means we have to come to terms with our past, forgiving and growing past the hurts of childhood, the failures of adulthood, and the pain we endure because we are human.

We have to take steps to ensure that we perceive correctly, in tune with the universe. We have to let go of our prejudices and our selfishness. We have to overcome our low self esteem, our hidden angers, and the fears which plague us. In short our spirituality needs to be both true and practical.

Visualization or Declaration

There's a sense in which visualization, "the act of visualizing," that is, "to see or form a mental image of," actually comes at the beginning of creation, before we've opened the circle, as thought proceeds action. Recall that intent comes first. Visualization creates a picture of your intent.

In this case, though, I am using the term "visualization" to mean an inner sight of the completed action, that is the action, quality, or product that one wishes to manifest. If you've done your "homework" well you know what you want in a rather complete way and your heart and soul support the idea. The idea is no longer vague or tentative but has fullness. It's not a sketchy idea but more like a detailed painting or photograph.

Another way to look at this step in the process is to name that which you wish, describing it as fully as possible, not with just a noun or verb but with adjectives, adverbs, and phrases that, like the visualization, give a full picture of that which you seek. In either case, you have a picture of your creation that has breadth and depth, detail, color, feeling, texture, perhaps even smell and taste.

Here we find a difficulty. There is the real possibility that your desire is so pin-pointed that you are seeking a needle in a haystack. Your imagination, in that case, has begun to limit your possibilities to a target so small that you may never have the faith and the power to manifest it. Once again it is a matter of being careful what you pray for, since one can imagine that which in itself holds contradiction.

There may have been that in my quest to win the computer bid. While I was seeking success in that way, I also wanted happiness in my career. At the time I had never thought that I couldn't be happy selling computers. I never imagined that I could be more successful as a writer than a salesman. My intention, then, limited my possibilities, an outcome that my soul was not willing to allow me to experience.

For these reasons, it is wise to admit to wider possibilities and seek outcomes that bring objectives that fit into broader, rather than more restrictive, modes. So one might seek prosperity, rather than riches, health rather than cure, a peaceful resolution rather than the one you might want to enforce.

In any case, remain open to the possibility that what has to change most and probably first is you, that the transformation you seek is in yourself. Be ready to assent to that which is your highest good, not clinging to what you demand but surrendering instead to the Universe in which you find yourself.

The second to last step in this ritual is the hardest, as you wait for the result. In most cases that means that you have set the world in motion and only time, which requires patience, will tell how your actions will be made manifest. Your inspiration, your manifestation, your intention may not appear as soon as you'd like. Remember that the laws of nature are steadfast and that what has begun will continue, connected as it is to the universe, rooted in the past, seen in the present, and as yet having a future that only time will reveal.

Closing

So in gratitude I walk to the North, and then West, South, and East, thanking the Bull, the Serpent, the Lion, and the Eagle for being with us, telling them they are free to stay or go, that the circle is ended.

Reflecting on Philosophy In the Dungeon

There is the danger, of course, that a little bit of information is just enough to get you into trouble. For that reason, I have tried to say that you are your own teacher, that authenticity is what is needed, and that your faith need be guided by love.

There is an incredibly beautiful and productive unity between sex and spirit, body and soul, the animal and the divine. May you find it, know it fully, and live it always.

---

1   Pike, Albert, *Morals and Dogma*, page 845.
2   Bonewits, Isaac, *Real Magic*, Samuel Weiser, Inc., York Beach, Maine, 1989, page 258.
3   I'm sure I read this quote in his book, *Think*

and Grow Rich, Wilshire Book Co., Chatsworth, CA, 1999, but I couldn't find it. In any case, Sister Mary Margaret gave it to me as a Christmas present one year, framed as a reminder of what I could accomplish.

4   Carr-Gomm, Philip and Stephanie, *The Druid Animal Oracle*, Simon &Schuster Inc., New York, 1994, page 5.

5   Illustration by M. Tallgrass.

6   *Gay Soul,* page 202.

7   *Gay Soul,* page 178.

8   *Gay Soul,* page 201.

Chapter

After Words **13**

W ell, there you have it, or at least there you have an introduction to my personal philosophy and my experiences. What happens next?

This book can't answer that question, as the answer belongs to you and to you alone. I've not written these words to give you rules and dogmas. They aren't meant to be the final word or anything. They are simply offered as ideas and stories for your consideration, a springboard to your own thoughts and ideas, a finger pointing to some new ways of thinking, a guidepost along a path that you may or may not wish to take.

Use this book to reflect on your experiences. Think about how you have grown. Consider how rose-colored your beliefs might be, how your self-image works or doesn't work for you.

Spend time each week reflecting on your goals, your desires, and your accomplishments. Perhaps you could journal or find a friend who will listen.

Let this book continue your journey. If some of the topics have interested you, explore them further. Study them, Try them. Discuss them with others. Prove them to yourself.

Whatever you do, have fun in the process. Be well and laugh often.

Jack Rinella
Chicago, June 2006

Acknowledgements

$\mathbf{W}$hen a sixty-year old writes about his spiritual
life, one that began with his baptism as an infant the week he
was born, there is a lot of personal history that reminds him of all
those whom he ought to acknowledge as part of that history. In
writing this book I have been reminded of nearly everyone I've
known, from my parents Rose Marie and Joe, and my Godparents
Aunt Margaret and Uncle Mike, all the way to my two-year old
grandson Liam, who gave meaning and purpose to every word
written herein.

The footnotes acknowledge those whom I have cited but
special mention goes to those whose books have touched me in a
special way: Alan Watts, Brugh Joy, MD, and Mark Thompson.
Their words were both inspirational and affirming. The Muses
used them well. Thanks, too, go to TammyJo Eckhart for her loyal
critique as a reader of my manuscripts and to Christine Pfeiffer for
her excellent editing.

Sister Mary Margaret encouraged me to meditate and
Conrad taught me how; in this venture my friend Ronn and my
lover at-the-time Steven were instrumental as well.

To the Christians, of many denominations, the Jews, and
the Pagans who shared with me their wisdom, I am in great debt,
especially Peter, who showed me my first circle, Brother Romulus
who taught me to garden, and Brother Joseph and Sister Mary
Carmel who both taught me how to be a professional writer. I am
in debt to Henry Fairbanks, PhD, a good friend and mentor while
I was in college. Thanks go as well to Ann for introducing me to

the Spirit of God in a living way and to the members of both St. Peter's Prayer Group and Love Inn for making the New Testament real.

I want to thank Matthew for his courage to believe in me and for the lessons he shared with me in the writing of this book. And thanks as well to those who stuck with me through and after those years of dark nights of my soul, especially Lynn Schornick, James Cappleman, Vince DiFruscio, Tom Stabnicky, Chuck Renslow, and Joel Beaver.

My partner of more than ten years, Patrick Herlihy, most of all, deserves acknowledgement for his long-term and continuing support and encouragement of my life and my work. Without him and many others I would have a lot less magic in my life.

Brain Waves A

Appendix

Since I am no authority on such phenomena, let me quote at length from Inteligen Inc., a Michigan-based company whose website at http://brain.web-us.com/brain wavesfunction. htm contains the following information:

> There are four categories ... of brain waves, ranging from the most activity to the least activity. When the brain is aroused and actively engaged in mental activities, it generates beta waves. These beta waves are of relatively low amplitude, and are the fastest of the four different brain waves... [ranging] from 15 to 40 cycles a second. Beta waves are characteristics of a strongly engaged mind. A person in active conversation would be in beta. A debater would be in high beta. A person making a speech, or a teacher, or a talk show host would all be in beta when they are engaged in their work.
>
> The next brain wave category in order of frequency is alpha. Where beta represented arousal, alpha represents non-arousal. Alpha brain waves are slower, and higher in amplitude. Their frequency ranges from 9 to 14 cycles per second. A person who has completed a task and sits down to rest is often in an alpha state. A person who takes time out to reflect or meditate is usually in an alpha state. A person who takes a break from a conference and walks in the garden is often in an alpha state.
>
> The next state, theta brain waves, are typically of even greater amplitude and slower

217

frequency... normally between 5 and 8 cycles a second. A person who has taken time off from a task and begins to daydream is often in a theta brain wave state. A person who is driving on a freeway, and discovers that they can't recall the last five miles, is often in a theta state--induced by the process of freeway driving. The repetitious nature of that form of driving compared to a country road would differentiate a theta state and a beta state in order to perform the driving task safely.

Individuals who do a lot of freeway driving often get good ideas during those periods when they are in theta. Individuals who run outdoors often are in the state of mental relaxation that is slower than alpha and when in theta, they are prone to a flow of ideas. This can also occur in the shower or tub or even while shaving or brushing your hair. It is a state where tasks become so automatic that you can mentally disengage from them. The ideation that can take place during the theta state is often free flow and occurs without censorship or guilt. It is typically a very positive mental state.

The final brain wave state is delta. Here the brain waves are of the greatest amplitude and slowest frequency. They typically center around a range of 1.5 to 4 cycles per second. They never go down to zero because that would mean that you were brain dead. But, deep dreamless sleep would take you down to the lowest frequency. Typically, 2 to 3 cycles a second.

Appendix

Endorphins B

Allow me to quote from an expert on the subject:

Endorphins, chemicals produced in the brain in response to a variety of stimuli, may be nature's cure for high levels of stress.

Discovered in 1975, endorphins are among the brain chemicals known as neurotransmitters, which function in the transmission of signals within the nervous system. At least 20 types of endorphins have been demonstrated in humans, and they may be located in the pituitary gland, other parts of the brain, or distributed throughout the nervous system.

Stress and pain are the two most common factors leading to the release of endorphins. Endorphins interact with the opiate receptors in the brain to reduce our perception of pain, having a similar action to drugs such as morphine and codeine. Unlike drugs, however, activation of the opiate receptors by the body's endorphins does not lead to addiction or dependence.

In addition to decreased feelings of pain, secretion of endorphins leads to feelings of euphoria, modulation of appetite, release of sex hormones, and enhancement of the immune response. With high endorphin levels, we feel less pain and fewer negative effects of stress. Endorphins have been suggested as modulators of the so-called "runner's high" that athletes achieve with prolonged exercise. While the role of endorphins and other compounds as potential triggers of this response has been debated

219

extensively in the literature, it is known that the body does produce endorphins in response to prolonged, continuous exercise.

Endorphin release varies among individuals -- meaning that two people who exercise at the same level or suffer the same degree of pain will not necessarily produce similar levels of endorphins. Certain foods, such as chocolate or chili peppers, can also lead to enhanced secretion of endorphins. In the case of chili peppers, the spicier the pepper, the more endorphins are secreted. The release of endorphins upon ingestion of chocolate likely explains the comforting feelings that many people associate with this food and the craving for chocolate in times of stress.

Even if you don't participate in strenuous athletics, you can also try activities that increase your body's endorphin levels. Studies of acupuncture and massage therapy have shown that both these techniques can stimulate endorphin secretion. Sex is also a potent trigger for endorphin release. Finally, the practice of meditation can increase the amount of endorphins released in your body. [1]

1   Stöppler, M.D., Melissa C., "Endorphins: The Body's Stress Fighters," found at http://stress.about.com/cs/exercise/a/aa072003a.htm on September 26, 2005.

Appendix

Suggested Readings C

I've read nearly a hundred books in order to write this one. The footnotes give you the sources I've quoted. More importantly you might want to read these suggested works, many of which are quoted in the text, as part of your own spiritual development. This then is not your usual "Suggested Readings" list but a chapter-by-chapter educational reading list.

BDSM

As I noted in my introductory disclaimer, there are many excellent books for those interested in learning about what it is that we (kinky folk) do. Though a book is no substitute for a good teacher and lots of practice, I will encourage readers to seek a few primers to our lifestyle. First, of course, I suggest my book *The Master's Manual*, Daedalus Publishing, Los Angeles, 1994. For those looking for a more definitive introduction to our culture, I suggest my book *Partners In Power*, Greenery Press, Oakland, CA, 2003.

For books about safe SM I heartedly endorse *Learning the Ropes* by Race Bannon, *SM 101* by Jay Wiseman, *The Loving Dominant* by John Warren, and *The New Topping Book* and *The New Bottoming Book*, both by Dossie Easton and Janet Hardy, Greenery Press. Two other very helpful and informative books are *Ties That Bind* by Guy Baldwin, Daedalus Publishing, and *Screw The Roses, Send Me the Thorns* by Philip Miller and Molly Devon, Mystic Rose Books, Mystic, CT 1988.

Introduction

If you haven't read the New Testament cover to cover, I suggest you do that, or at least read *The Gospel According to John* and *The Acts of the Apostles*. For Old Testament reading I suggest Robert Alter's new translation of *The Five Books of Moses* (W. W. Norton & Company, New York, 2004). If you really want to know more about the *Baltimore Catechism*, it can be found at http://www.catholic.net/rcc/Catechism/download/baltimore1.doc. For an excellent summation of Christianity see Alan Watt's *Myth and Ritual in Christianity* (Beacon Press, Boston, 1968).

If you're interested in my Pentecostal experiences, I would refer you to *Scott Free*, written by Scott Ross with John and Elizabeth Sherrill. I am called Joe (my actual first name) in that book (Chosen Books, 1976).

You also might want to read *Radical Ecstasy* by Janet Green and Dossie Easton (Greenery Press, 2005) as a starting point for your spiritual quest as they describe much of the psychic phenomena found in BDSM.

In the Beginning

You're going to find that I have relied a great deal on the several books of Classical History written by Thomas Cahill. For starters you might want to read *The Gifts of the Jews* (Anchor Books, Doubleday, New York, 1998). Another of his titles, *How the Irish Saved Civilization*, makes fascinating reading and will expand your historical paradigms as well.

An old favorite of mine is *Way of the Peaceful Warrior, A Book That Changes Lives* by Dan Millman (H.J. Kramer, Inc., Tiburon, CA, 1980).

222

It's All in Your --------

My first introduction to the biological processes involved in SM came from Geoff Mains' excellent book, *Urban Aboriginals* (Daedalus Publishing, Los Angeles, 2004). You will also find more information in Appendices A and B. I suggest you visit the websites cited there to learn more. If you can find a copy of Elmer Green's *Beyond Biofeedback* it will give you an excellent, though dated, introduction to these ideas.

Spirit As the Ancients Knew It

I can hardly teach you all the history you need to know, but again I will encourage you to read Thomas Cahill, specifically *Sailing the Wine-Dark Sea* (Anchor Books, New York, 2004) and *Desire of the Everlasting Hills: The World Before and After Jesus* (Anchor Books, New York, 1999). For Eastern Philosophy, I have relied upon the writings of Alan Watts, specifically *The Way of Zen* (Vintage Books, New York, 1957) and *The Watercourse Way* (Pantheon Books, New York, 1975).

Stephan Grundy's retelling of *Gilgamesh* (William Morrow, New York, 2000), is well worth reading. You might also be interested in Eknath Easwaran's translation and commentary on *The Bhagavad Gita* (Vintage Books, New York, 2000). Though it may be hard to find, Eliot Elisofon and Alan Watts have given us a very interesting photo book with commentary in *The Temple of Konarak, Erotic Spirituality* (Thames and Hudson, London, 1971) that documents the open sexuality of Tantric Hinduism.

For a better understanding of Dionysos, read *The God of Ecstasy, Sex Roles and the Madness of Dionysos* by Arthur Evans (St. Martin's Press, New York, 1988). For learning more about the Gnostics I highly recommend *The Gnostic Gospels* and *Beyond*

Belief, both by Elaine Pagels (Random House, New York).

Finally, among the plethora of literature on Tantra, I suggest the two volume set *Principles of Tantra*, by Sir John Woodroffe writing as Arthur Avalon (Ganesh & Co., 1978). Though it is sometimes hard to work your way through all the Sanskrit names and terms, it is a very complete presentation. Lastly you might find Marvin W. Meyer's *The Ancient Mysteries, A Sourcebook* (Harper & Row, San Francisco, 1987) an interesting introduction to alternative religious thinking.

The Power Exchange

To begin, I highly and emphatically suggest Dr. Brugh Joy's book, *Joy's Way, A Map for the Transformational Journey* (Jeremy P. Tarcher, Inc., Los Angeles, 1979). It has been transformational in my life and his understanding of energy is basic to my personal spirituality. For the book that started me out on my understanding of meditation and creative visualization, I suggest Shakti Gawain's *Creative Visualization: Use the Power of Your Imagination to Create What You Want in Your Life* (25th anniversary edition, published by New World Library, 2002). Further information can be found in Avalon's *The Serpent Power, The Secrets of Tantric and Shakti Yoga* (Dove Publications, New York, 1974). Another hard to find book and excellent book is *At the Feet of the Master* by Krishnamurti (Yogi Publication Society, Chicago, undated).

A Pause to Reflect

The most important book you can read on this topic is written in your heart.

Unity

Here you'll have to go back to the books by Alan Watts,

especially *The Book On the Taboo Against Knowing Who You Are*, Vintage Books, New York, 1989.

Life As Process

I have to refer you to my book *Partners In Power* (Greenery Press, Oakland, CA, 2003). For an understanding of sadomasochism, see *Dark Eros, the Imagination of Sadism* by Thomas Moore (Spring Publications, Woodstock, CT, 1990 and for life process his book, *Dark Nights of the Soul* (Gotham Books, New York, 2005).

Life In Stages

I found *Rites and Symbols of Initiation* (Harper & Row, New York, 1958) by Mircea Eliade, fascinating and very informative about primitive initiation rites. I highly recommend *Man's Search For Meaning* by Viktor Frankl (Washington Square Press, New York, 1984).

According to Your Faith

Better read the New Testament for yourself, but please have an open mind. I can also recommend *Think and Grow Rich* by Napoleon Hill (Wilshire Book Co., Chatsworth, CA, 1999).

True Spirituality

Mark Thompson's book, *Gay Soul, Finding the Heart of Gay Spirit and Nature* (HarperCollins, 1995), was invaluable in my writing of this book and I highly recommend it to you. Sri Aurobindo has written much about Eastern Spirituality. The compilation of his lectures, found in *The Riddle of This World* (Sri Aurobindo Ashram, Pondicherry, India, circa 1933) is only one of many books to consult.

Practical Spirituality

An amazing book about contemporary Tantra is *The TantraMan Letters* by Victor Bliss and Nathan James (www. XLibris.com, 2002).

Magic

Most of what is in this chapter comes out of my own experience and I take the blame for all of it. You will find *The Ceremonial Circle* by Sedonia Cahill and Joshua Halpern helpful (HarperSanFrancisco, 1990). See also Isaac Bonewits' *Real Magic* for another view of what is magical (Samuel Weiser, Inc., York Beach, ME, 1989).

Index ■

NaNactions, responsibility for, 23
Alter, Robert, 10
altered states, 191, 207–209
ancient Greece, 43–47, 78
anger, 134–135
animal totems, 197–198
Aurobindo (Indian mystic), 36, 166–168, 169
authentic self, 174–175, 183
Avalon, Arthur, 51, 68
    awakenings
    dangers in, 130–131
    definition of, 129–130
    initiations and, 125–128
    Kundalini experiences, 126, 127
Bacchus, 45–47, 91
balance, 77–78, 168–169
Baldwin, Guy, 117–118
baptism, 127
BDSM
    beliefs and, 137–141
    bodies and, 19–20
    bondage, 85
    as consensual activity, 12
    cultures and, 56–58
    education in, 106–107, 121
    experiences of, 85–86, 126–127
    flogging, 86
    initiation practices, 55–56
    kinky sex as, 46
    paradigms and, 10–13
    power exchanges and, 68–71
    reasons for, 138
    roles of mind in, 18
    spanking, 139–140
    spirituality and, 174–175
    stages in, 123–124
    subculture influence of, 81
    trust between student and instructor, 109
    see also mind, spirit and spirituality
BDSM scenes
    altered states in, 163–164
    comfortable space, creation of, 193
    meditation between partners and, 183
    negotiations in, 70–71, 138–139
    processes of, 104–105

227

228

About the Author

For more than fourteen years Jack Rinella has been writing LeatherViews, a weekly column about his favorite topic: kinky sex. The acclaimed author of the best-selling book, *The Master's Manual*, as well as *The Compleat Slave, Partners in Power, Toybag Guide to Clips and Clamps*, and *Becoming a Slave*, is a free-lance writer and college instructor. A sought-after lecturer, Jack has presented seminars on BDSM history, techniques, and relationships across the country including the Leather Leadership Conference, Black Rose, Bash at the Beach, Beat Me in St. Louis, TES, Headspace in Bloomington, IN, PEER in Cincinnati, and the Arizona Power Exchange.

Born in Albany, New York of Italian-American parents, he's been a high school and college teacher, a drug rehabilitation counselor, a cook, a computer salesman, a Catholic seminarian, a Pentecostal minister, an advertising copy writer, a graphic designer, and has done stints at printing, publishing, telemarketing, head-hunting, and computer consulting. He has a Bachelor's degree in Philosophy and a Master's Degree in Business Administration.

He has been active in the Leather scene since 1983, is a founding member of MAsT-Chicago, an associate member of the Chicago Hellfire Club, and serves as a director on the board of the Leather Leadership Conference. He has written extensively about our lifestyle as a weekly columnist for Gay Chicago Magazine. His writing has also appeared in Drummer Magazine, in The (San Francisco) Sentinel, and in Philadelphia Gay News, and is available on-line at his website at http://www.LeatherViews.com and through his free weekly newsletter which can be subscribed to on his website.

He lives on the North side of Chicago with his partner of more than ten years, Patrick, and Matthew, where he passes the time writing, cruising, and falling in love whenever he can. You can contact Jack at mrjackr@Leathermail.com.